Keepsakes

Using Family Stories in Elementary Classrooms

Linda Winston

Heinemann
Portsmouth, NH

HEINEMANN
A division of Reed Elsevier Inc.
361 Hanover Street
Portsmouth, NH 03801-3912
Offices and agents throughout the world

The author and publisher wish to thank those who have generously given permission to reprint borrowed material:

Excerpts reprinted from "Mrs. Rainey's Grandma" by Christian McEwen by permission of Teachers & Writer's Collaborative, 5 Union Square West, New York, New York, 10003. Copyright 1995.
Thanks to Henry Street Settlement House and Community School District One in New York City for permission to quote part of "Nickie's Story" from *Parents Have Stories to Tell*, 1994, Vol. IV:30.
Fig. 8-1: Organized Charity: Family Making Artificial Flowers. Photograph by Jessie Tarbox Beals, the Jacob A. Riis Collection, Museum of the City of New York.

Library of Congress Cataloging-in-Publication Data

Winston, Linda.
   Keepsakes: using family stories in elementary classrooms / Linda Winston.
      p.   cm.
   Includes bibliographical references.
   ISBN 0–435–07235–8 (alk. paper)
    1. Storytelling—United States.   2. Education, Elementary—Parent participation—United States.   3. Family—United States—Folklore.
4. Family—Study and teaching (Elementary)—United States.
5. Language arts (Elementary)—United States.   I. Title.
LB1042.W56 1997
372.67′7—DC21

                96–49364
                CIP

Editor: *William Varner*
Production: *J. B. Tranchemontagne*
Manufacturing: *Louise Richardson*
Book design: *Jenny Jensen Greenleaf*
Cover design: *Mary Cronin*
Cover art: *Pamela Crimmins and Lucinda Gable*

Printed in the United States of America on acid-free paper
06 05 04 03 VP 6 7 8 9

I once told a friend that families were like minefields, that we walk and dance through them never knowing where or when something or someone is going to explode. Though I haven't lived in the same city as my mother for over twenty years, I can still go home to Cleveland, walk in her front door, and within hours begin to feel like the fourteen-year-old I once was, rebelling against my mother's control. Next to the image of the minefield, I have, as a result of reading and editing these stories and poems about family, added another: family as a living mystery, constantly changing, constantly providing us clues about who we are, and demanding that we recognize the new and challenging shapes it often takes. We are, of course, central players in that mystery.

—MARY HELEN WASHINGTON
Memory of Kin: Stories About Family By Black Writers

Contents

Foreword

Linda Winston's *Keepsakes: Using Family Stories in Elementary Classrooms* is a family treasure that I encourage every teacher to read. When I first started leafing through the pages, I found myself totally immersed in *Keepsakes*. Perhaps because I was writing a story about my own family, I felt I was both literally and figuratively—through the story I was writing, through my teaching, through my research, through my philosophical beliefs and theories—standing beside Linda Winston, agreeing with what she had written and continually saying to myself "I wish I had written that." The book begins by inviting the readers to share our own "cultural biographies, as a way to develop some understanding of the various cultures we, ourselves, represent." As we read *Keepsakes*, we are encouraged to embark on our own explorations, and then share the findings together. For me, *Keepsakes* became a very personal journey.

When I was a little girl my mother and I used to travel on a train from Ashford in Kent to Pontypool in South Wales. From there we took a bus to my grandparents' village which was called Garn-yr-eu. The Garn, as we called it, translated into English means "a heap of stones." And that's what it was, four rows of tiny tar-covered miners' houses, each with two rooms up and two rooms down and a lavatory out the back, all surrounded by the giant heaps of slag brought up from the earth by the coal miners. Each summer I spent about two months playing with the local children in the "hills" behind my Nan and Grandad's house. We played "house" by arranging stones to make rooms and by collecting bits of broken crockery that had been thrown away with the other rubbish behind the chicken coops and pigeon lofts. We slid down the slag heaps on pieces of cardboard and dropped stones down old mine shafts.

But now the Garn is now quite literally "a heap of stones." It was bull-dozed to the ground and all that is left are the curbstones—just enough of them for us to work out the place where my grandparents' house once stood. Just before I read *Keepsakes* for the first time, I had traveled to Wales with my mother and we parked our car on the spot where the house in which she grew up had stood. We ate sandwiches and talked about the Garn that we had known. We retold stories that we both knew by heart, and we laughed at silly things as we made our journey into the past. And although there were many difficult times in the Garn, my mother says that she only remembers the sun shining when she was a child and I, too, remember only sunny days.

My mother is the last one in our family of her generation. Moreover, she is one of the last inhabitants of the village who is still alive. It concerns me that she has no contemporaries who can share with her the experience of growing up in that Welsh coal-mining village, that my children have grown up so far away from it, and that this rich heritage of experience will be lost to them and their children. Like so many other families, our connections have been broken between the generations. In a way we—my family and many other families in America—have been cast adrift and separated from the past. We are left only with the present and our identities are deeply affected by the breaking. The important continuous threads that stretch back through the generations to our grandparents and great-grandparents and forward to our children and grandchildren are broken.

This is why *Keepsakes* is such an important book. Linda Winston has gathered together the stories of the teachers and students in New York schools who have made family studies central to their curriculum. She helps us understand how important it is that we provide all our students and their families with ways to explore their own family heritage, and how we can knit the broken threads together into brilliantly colored tapestries which hold all our histories. She shows us how by providing many varied examples of family studies that we can use as a basis for our own personal explorations, and then as the basis for beginning family studies in our classrooms.

Both here and abroad, "family literacy" programs have been developed based for years on the underlying assumption that the home environments of the children we teach provide neither the literacy tools nor the personal support which might enable children to "make up" their deficits. "Fixing" the family has become big business. Family literacy programs have induction activities, intake procedures, and strategies for retention, and in one publication I even read that for many families becoming literate would mean changing attitudes, values, and even cultures. Recently in the United States and in many other countries, the focus on family has changed significantly.

In 1994, at an International Forum on Family Literacy, educators from around the world worked together to develop an international declaration of principles which we hope will help to shift the rhetoric of the family literacy movement to more positive and realistic ways of talking about and working with families. Our intent was to support families, to emphasize that the opportunity to become literate is a human right, and to encourage families and communities to create their own community-based family literacy activities.

The documentation we developed at the forum became the basis for discussion among educators throughout the world, and eventually for a book entitled *Many Families, Many Literacies: An International Declaration of Principles*. Its very first principle is that families have the right to define themselves—as they do in *Keepsakes*.

As I move back and forth between *Many Families, Many Literacies* and *Keepsakes*, I am struck by the extraordinary images that Linda Winston creates of teachers who deeply respect and care for the families of the children they teach. Many of the principles developed at the international forum are also the foundation of the family studies that *Keepsakes* describes. In the classrooms of the teachers we meet in *Keepsakes*, families *do* define themselves, literacy *is* a human right, and *all* languages have an equal potential to convey the full range of human thought and experience. *Keepsakes* is both wise and wonderful. It is a gentle book with a powerful message. The everyday lives of families, their social histories and cultural biographies are the foundation of every child's school experience. Now it is up to us to learn from the teachers whose stories Linda Winston tells, and to develop our own family studies in both our classrooms and our schools.

—*Denny Taylor*

Acknowledgments

Before I thank the people who contributed directly to this book, I want to acknowledge those whose examples have inspired me: scholars and educators who created the intellectual and social settings in which I met and worked with nearly all the caring, imaginative, resolute teachers whose practices inform these pages. For showing me that schoolrooms can be roomy enough to include the important people and events in children's out-of-school lives, I am grateful to Lucy Calkins and her colleagues at the Columbia University Teachers College Writing Project; Amanda Dargan and Lonetta Gaines, codirectors of The Center for Folk Arts in Education at Bank Street College; Susan Fleminger, director of Arts in Education at the Henry Street Settlement; Judith Pasamanick and her colleagues from the NEH Folklore Institutes at Bank Street College; Susan Perlstein, director of Elders Share the Arts; Augustus Trowbridge, director of Manhattan Country School; Elaine Wickens of Bank Street College; and Steven Zeitlin, director of City Lore.

There are two people whose counsel I most often sought throughout the writing of this book: Jacqueline Lynch, who has given me the blessings of her friendship and her insights as teacher and parent ever since she taught one of my children in her kindergarten class a generation ago, and my daughter, Valerie Gutwirth, once Jacqueline's kindergarten pupil and now her colleague and friend who has generously shared with me the process and results of her work in the Family Study at Manhattan Country School. When I needed some response from other knowledgeable readers, I turned to four people, asking each to read in a specific capacity: Stanley Braham as friend and editor of my earliest, sloppiest copies; Muriel Hammer as mentor and colleague in anthropology; Ruth Shapiro as friend and fellow teacher; and Hella Winston as researcher and photographer.

School principals and staff made it possible for me to carry out the observations and interviews for the book. Augustus Trowbridge, founding director of Manhattan Country School, and his colleagues, Lois Gelernt and Michele Sola, have my warm thanks for lighting the way to Family Study and graciously supporting my work. My warmest thanks also go to these principals and their colleagues from other schools mentioned in these pages: Regina Birdsell and Pat Muggleston of Academy Elementary School in Madison, Connecticut; Judith Chin and Janet Won, P.S. 124 Manhattan; Yves Douglas and her colleagues, Yvonne Gunn and Steven Mohney, P.S. 3 Brooklyn; Jean Marie Finnerty and Maria Velez Clarke, The Children's Workshop School in Manhattan; Gary Goldstein, P.S. 199 Manhattan; Leonard Golubchick, P.S. 20 Manhattan; Jane Hand, P.S. 87 Manhattan; Roberta Kirshbaum, P.S. 75 Manhattan; Ivan Kushner, P.S. 19 Manhattan; Gloria Wagner and her colleagues, Debbi Aizenstain, Jill Benedict, Susan Maloney, and Karen Mehler, P.S. 24 Queens.

Linda Greengrass and Gary Zingher are the children's librarians who provided invaluable suggestions for the bibliography of picture books. The Child Study Children's Book Committee at Bank Street College kindly permitted me to quote many of the annotations from their annual lists in my bibliography of picture books that support the family stories curriculum.

I will always remember the faces and voices of the children who generously shared their thoughts, their feelings, and their work with me. To the parents who made me feel welcome in their storytelling workshops, agreed to be interviewed, and gave permission to include their own and/or their children's work in this book, I owe special thanks.

William Varner, my editor at Heinemann, encouraged and accompanied me—via countless letters, telephone calls, and e-mail messages—every step of the way. I wholeheartedly acknowledge my gratitude to him with affection and respect. Thank you to Joanne Tranchemontagne for the care she took in shepherding the book through the production process.

Tracy Lee has my warmest thanks for her intelligent, careful typing of the final manuscript.

The people who have been most in my thoughts as I wrote are my family, especially my brother and my children, who have taught me that being part of a family is sometimes difficult and stressful but always filled with color, comfort, laughter, and joy.

Finally, in considering how best to express my deep appreciation to the teachers without whose work this book would not exist, I invited them to introduce themselves, individually, in the extended acknowledgments that directly follow these.

The Teachers

Laura Daigen's master's thesis at Bank Street College of Education provided the basis for, and continues to inform, Manhattan Country School's pioneering Family Study curriculum. Currently, she coordinates the Spanish department at Central Park East Seconday Schools and consults to a network of alternative schools in New York City (Introduction, Chapter 1, Chapter 2).

Dawn C. Formey holds an M.F.A. in theatre from Ohio State University. She is an actress, a drama workshop coordinator for Elders Share the Arts, and an adjunct instructor at the College of New Rochelle, Brooklyn campus.

Kit Fung facilitates workshops for principals, teachers, and students in New York City and teaches courses in multicultural bilingual education at Adelphi University. Fluent in Cantonese, Toisanese, and Mandarin, she also incorporates the languages of dance and storytelling in her work with children in the classroom (Chapter 4).

Valerie Gutwirth cotaught the Family Study curriculum at Manhattan Country School for three years, beginning with the year she received her master's degree from Bank Street College of Education. She is currently project coordinator of the Multicultural Curriculum Program at Children's Hospital in Oakland, California (Introduction, Chapter 1, Chapter 2).

Junius Harris is a sixth-grade teacher at Manhattan Country School, where he has been teaching about families and the civil rights movement for ten years (Introduction, Chapter 1, Chapter 2).

Scott Hirschfeld, a fourth-grade teacher at P.S. 87 in Manhattan, has taught in the New York City public school system for ten years. Committed to global education, he was a Fulbright exchange teacher; recently, he has been featured in *It's Elementary*, a documentary film aimed at combating homophobia in the primary school (Chapter 2).

Ted Kesler teaches at the third-grade level at P.S. 75 in Manhattan; besides teaching, he enjoys playing music, writing, performing, playing tennis, running marathons, and watching NBA basketball. For him teaching is "mostly a dialogue between teacher and student"; he is never likely to repeat the same curriculum in the same way, not even the one featured in this book (Chapter 6).

Robin Kruter's appetizing food curriculum for first graders at P.S. 24 in Queens helps children in her classroom learn about and enjoy their own and their classmates' cultures (Chapter 5).

Beth Maloney's background in improvisational comedy and her teaching experience inform her work in docent training and programming at the education department of the Museum of the City of New York. She graduated from Swarthmore College in spring 1995 and will soon complete her master's degree in education at Bank Street College (Chapter 8).

Christian McEwen is a published writer and teacher with a special interest in nature writing and a family memoir. Her anthology *Tomboys* will be published by Beacon Press in spring 1997 (Chapter 2).

Pat Muggleston, language arts specialist at Academy Elementary School in Madison, Connecticut, and fifth-grade teachers Wilma Maus, Mary Paffrath, and Mary Anne Steele read, write, laugh, and work well together as a team (Chapter 8).

Charlotte Norris, a primary-grade teacher at P.S. 199 in Manhattan, is a member of the Leadership Project at the Teachers College Writing Project (Chapter 4).

Krina Patel teaches Family Study to seven- and eight-year-olds at Manhattan Country School. She has also taught children with special needs and has written about using the arts in the elementary curriculum (Introduction, Chapter 1, Chapter 2).

Mary C. Savage, founder of the Henry Street Settlement Parent Storytelling Workshop, is a storyteller, teacher, and writer who uses storytelling as a context for building multicultural understanding. Her forthcoming *Seed Stories for Multicultural Times* (in press) highlights the liberatory dimensions of storytelling (Chapter 3).

Joanne Schultz, intergenerational coordinator for Elders Share the Arts, has led workshops in oral history and theater with older adults and intergenerational groups throughout New York City since 1985. She has also conceived and directed innovative theater productions for the Ninth Street Theater, which have also played at Theater for the New City and Performance Space 122 (Chapter 7).

Jenny Tuten has taught children, teenagers, and adults for more than fifteen years in public and independent schools in New York, New Jersey, and England. Besides teaching, her passions include music, her husband, and her daughter (Chapter 5).

Cheryl Tyler teaches kindergarten at P.S. 75 in Manhattan. She is a member of the Leadership Project at the Teachers College Writing Project (Chapter 3).

Evelyn Weisfeld's family history project at Booker T. Washington Middle School in Manhattan, published in her curriculum guides and her *Book of Life*, encourages teachers, students, and families throughout the city to share their stories; her work has influenced all the chapters of this book.

Gary Zingher, codeveloper and coteacher of the Creative Library Programs course at Bank Street College of Education, utilized his experience in both writing and creative dramatics while working as librarian at Manhattan Country School. His book *At the Pirate Academy*, published by the American Library Association in 1990, describes his highly creative vision of library programming (Preface to the Picture Book Bibliography).

Telling Our Stories

Everyone has a story to tell,
if only someone would listen,
if only someone would ask.

—William Zimmerman

This book has its origins in the kaleidoscope of stories we tell and retell in my family. The idea for the book began to take shape in 1990, when I participated in some workshops at the Teachers College Writing Project at Columbia University. There a small group of teachers learned of my background as a researcher in cultural anthropology. They asked me to help them gain some insights into the wide range of cultures represented by the children in their classrooms. In response, I suggested that we begin by sharing our own "cultural autobiographies" as a way to develop some understanding of the various cultures we represented.

To illustrate what I meant by "cultural autobiography," I gave each colleague a copy of Kathryn Morgan's stories (Morgan 1976; 1980) about her great grandmother Caddy's experiences in slavery. Transmitted orally across four generations, these stories, which Morgan calls Caddy Buffers because they serve as critical ego supports or "buffers" against the world outside her family, continue to guide and inspire her. "Frankly," she writes, "Caddy comes to my rescue even now when some obstacle seems insurmountable to me." After we had read and discussed Morgan's stories, we decided to meet again several weeks later to share some of our own.

1

A surprising intimacy soon developed among us as we read our family stories to each other. My favorite story described the special feelings of an Italian-American teacher's family for their mother. She told us how, at some point during every family gathering, her grandfather would say "Ma-ma," smacking his lips in an exaggerated kiss to remind his children and grand-children that "Mama is the only word in the language with two kisses in it." "Ma-ma, Ma-ma" the rest of us mouthed silently, tasting the meaning of "mother" in Italian-American culture.

My contribution to our exchange of family stories focused on the ones my maternal grandfather told me, in installments, when I was about six years old. The main character of each installment was a girl my age, whom my grandfather called Leah-the-Forsaken. The girl invariably broke a moral rule that led her friends and family to reject her, one by one, when they discovered her infraction of it. As each episode ended, Leah was once again "forsaken." Only in adulthood did I come to understand that the Leah stories were my grandfather's way of passing on to me some of the most important teachings of Judaism. Although I continually implored him to "tell me another," there was something daunting about the stories. What I remember best, though, is not the scariness of the stories but, rather, the warmth and reassurance of my grandfather's presence.

The powerful experience of exchanging family stories with my colleagues made me realize that such an exchange had the potential of creating the same sense of connection and community among children, their families, and their teachers. Excited by the possibility, I began doing research on how teachers were using family stories.

I learned that since 1966, when Elliott Wigginton began a magazine called *Foxfire* with his pupils in a small public high school in rural Georgia, many U.S. teachers have been sending their students out to collect stories from their families and neighbors. More recently, such books as *A Celebration of American Family Folklore* (Zeitlin, Kotkin, and Baker 1982) and Elizabeth Simons' *Student Worlds, Student Words* (1990) on teaching writing through folklore have shown junior high and high school English and Social Studies teachers how to use family stories as teaching resources. Yet neither of these books specifically addresses the topic of how family stories are used in the elementary school. In the literature of the teaching of writing to young children, there are some references to children's writing on family topics (Calkins and Harwayne 1991), and Sara Mosle (1995) shows how movingly her third graders shared their family stories with her in dialogue journals that she wrote with them. But, with two notable exceptions—*Nuestro Mundo*, Laura Diagen's (1981) thesis for Bank Street College of Education, and the groundbreaking applied anthropology projects conducted by Carlos Velez-Ibanez and his colleagues (1992, 1995) with Mexican-American, Native

American, and African-American children, their families, and teachers—I have found no work that names and celebrates family stories as a powerful curricular theme in the early grades. That void is what this book sets out to fill.

Questioning the notion of an ideal "Everyfamily," that is, shattering myths that deny the complexities of family life as many of us experience it today, the teachers and pupils I observed and interviewed are learning how the idea of family is constantly changing. In the process, they are discovering that what we remember and pass on becomes an essential part of family.

The definition of *family story* that has evolved as I gathered material for this book is roomier than the traditional folklorist's definition that, in Steve Zeitlin's words, includes "any incident retold by one family member about another over a period of years."(1982:10) My definition also includes cautionary tales, folk tales, fairy tales, and the kinds of bedtime stories some parents make up for their young children each night, based on a recounting of a child's own day. Family expressions, sayings, customs, keepsakes, photographs, recipes, holidays, and celebrations also belong here.

Our family stories reflect our strengths. In the inner city, however, they may not focus exclusively on such topics as how a child's forebears came to America or how a family moved to the big city. Instead, there may be tragic tales of drive-by shootings, crack addicts, homelessness, or abuse. Although no such traumatic stories emerged in the classrooms described here, teachers will need to consider how best to respond to those who feel their experiences are so painful that it is better to forget them. Sometimes a teacher working with family stories will collaborate with a school psychologist or social worker (Krogness 1994; Roberts 1994). Others may arrange to link children with surrogate parents or grandparents, sometimes with the help of intergenerational programs such as Elders Share the Arts. Most of us will find reassurance in the work of Zeitlin and his colleagues who report that harrowing and traumatic experiences tend to become integrated into the ongoing life of a family when they are turned into stories (Zeitlin 1993–94:15). Indeed, making such experiences into stories may be what keeps us from being damaged by them.

Using family stories preventively, to diminish stress between children and parents, was an aspect of Cornell University's Family Portraits Program, which concerned itself, in part, with developing approaches to reducing the risk of child abuse. In several New York City school districts, Cornell's storytelling workshops for parents and teachers became so popular that parents whose children attend elementary schools enrolled in them for the pleasure of learning to tell stories in their children's classrooms. Others participated in the parent storytelling workshops offered by Henry Street Settlement's Arts in Education program. Some parents skip the formal preparation and simply visit their children's classes, usually in pairs, to share traditional tales and family stories.

As research in linguistics and anthropology clearly shows, stories that people tell about remembered or projected experiences belong to a fundamental genre in every sociocultural group; they are also central to the acquisition of literacy (Heath 1982; 1983; 1986a; 1986b). Contributing in natural and spontaneous ways to the development of literacy in young children, family stories and oral histories enliven and enrich the elementary curriculum. For one thing, they give children a direct connection with the past, a sense of history. When one parent visited his daughter's kindergarten class at P.S. 75, on Manhattan's upper West Side, he brought along a quilt made by her great-great-great-grandmother. The children listened with amazement when he told them it was made from old pajamas, outgrown shirts, and "stuff like that." "People actually did something in the winter before there was television," this father told the children. The teacher, who has been inviting families to tell stories to her kindergarten youngsters since 1991, emphasizes that "parents bring in a diversity of experience I could never bring by myself."

A third grade teacher at P.S. 75 draws on family stories to introduce the study of immigration. "My classroom is a little United Nations," he says. "We come from more than a dozen different countries—or our parents do— and so these children should know about immigration. Their own family stories give them a direct connection with it, and that's important to children of this age who are still concrete and egocentric."

At Manhattan Country School (MCS), which has maintained a racially, ethnically, and economically mixed group of pupils, teachers, and staff since its inception, defining the concept of "family" is key to the Family Study curriculum for seven- and eight-year-olds. It is the big narrative underlying all the other family stories. "Throughout Family Study," says a teacher who taught the curriculum for three years, "children learn to answer the question, 'What is a family?'" At the beginning of the year, a child in one group agonized, "I don't have a family. It's just me and my mom." Two months later she joked that she would be doing the homework for weeks because she had to write about so many people in her family. She had learned to answer the question "What is a Family?" by saying "*Mine* is. But mine isn't the only way or the best (or worst) way. Look at all these ways of being a family!"

Families with parents living apart in different households, families that are homeless, families headed by gay or lesbian parents—to give just a few examples—challenge teachers to open a dialogue with their elementary school pupils about the range of existing family structures. This book does not attempt to give a comprehensive treatment of family structure. It does suggest, however, useful and accessible resources for teachers and children that include many of the family themes and configurations that may be represented in today's classrooms. Whatever the challenges, the teachers whose work is described here feel that a family stories program is worth doing, for the sake of the children.

Recent studies indicate that conversation between parents and children is rare in today's homes (Schwartz 1995). Time spent talking about substantive issues—as opposed to giving commands or criticisms—may be as little as eight minutes a weekday for a father and his offspring; working mothers communicate with their children eleven minutes or less a weekday. Teachers can stimulate positive interaction and conversation at home by engaging children and their families in a family stories project.

Working on family stories teaches young children primary research skills: interviewing, recording, and organizing information gathered from interviews; letter writing; mapping; collecting family "artifacts"; creating family museums; and dramatizing and celebrating family history in a variety of ways. These hands-on activities are particularly appropriate in the early elementary grades. Children who may not be ready to use books as major sources for research can begin to experience the excitement of the research process through primary sources.

Involving families in the educational lives of their children; building community among parents, children, teachers, school staff, and administrators; making a positive impact on children's literacy development; giving both children and adults a sense of their familial and cultural heritage—these are some of the major rewards of bringing family stories to the classroom.

Teachers who want to develop a successful family stories curriculum in the elementary grades have many exciting resources at hand. Educators are using stories in many innovative ways and have much to say about the role of storytelling in theory and in practice (Bruner 1986;1990; Dyson and Genishi 1994; Paley 1990; 1992). In response to the Foxfire project, a diversity of magazines that publish particular family stories has sprung up across the country and includes Eskimo, Navaho, Mexican-American, Choctaw, and Cajun traditions. Information about these magazines can be obtained from the National Storytelling Association (NSA). Storytelling festivals are held all over the United States and feature family storytellers, many of whom are available to work in schools; their lively books and tapes can also be ordered from the NSA. Centers for folk arts and culture, such as the City Lore/Bank Street College Center for Folk Arts in Education, work closely with teachers. Local libraries and museums provide access to useful oral history projects. The appendices to this book include annotated bibliographies of these and other resources for teachers, most of which are mentioned in the context of describing the classrooms and projects that are featured in the following chapters.

What follows in these pages draws mainly, though not exclusively, on my fieldwork in New York City schools. This work makes no claim to be representative of all elementary classrooms in the United States, but it does include classrooms in both public and private schools, in urban and suburban settings. The first two chapters focus primarily on the work of several teachers at Manhattan Country School, where the Family Study curriculum for second graders began more than fifteen years ago and has continued to the present. For the past eight years, through a series of weekend workshops, teachers from MCS have shared the curriculum with public school teachers in the New York metropolitan area and in other parts of the country. Some former MCS teachers have also taken teaching and/or administrative positions in public schools; in collaboration with mentors at MCS, they are adapting the Family Study program to these new settings.

Chapter 3 describes parent storytelling workshops developed by Cornell University and by the Henry Street Settlement's Arts in Education program in several New York City school districts; its focus is on parents at four different schools who tell stories in kindergarten classrooms. Chapter 4 compares two first grade classrooms, one in Chinatown and the other on the Upper West Side of Manhattan. In the former, adults on the school staff tell their own family stories to first graders and encourage the children's parents and grandparents to share theirs. In the latter, family stories emerge when teachers introduce the children to the study of memoir.

Chapter 5 records the experience of fourth graders who share family stories in the context of a cooking project. Chapter 6 describes a third grade classroom in which family storytellers make an important contribution to the children's study of immigration. An intergenerational theater project that brings together children in the third and fifth grades with senior citizens from the neighborhoods surrounding their schools is described in Chapter 7. In the final chapter, descriptions of two fifth grade projects—one in New York City's Tenement Museum, and the other in a suburban Connecticut school—feature family photography.

An annotated bibliography of picture books that support the family stories curriculum follows the final chapter. It is introduced with a brief preface by Gary Zingher, whose work as the librarian at Manhattan Country School included many years of library support for the Family Study curriculum. A list of other valuable resources for teachers is set forth in a second bibliography.

Building a family stories curriculum will challenge a teacher. There is no manual or guide to follow. The scope and sequence, as Mary Mercer Krogness (1987) has suggested, are "as unpredictable as families themselves" and will depend entirely on the interests and comfort of the students and their kin. In the pages that follow I invite you to explore the world of family stories and create your own guidelines for using them in your classroom, as you and your students shape and are shaped by the stories themselves.

1
Getting Started

There should be a sign above every classroom door that reads, "All teachers who enter, be prepared to tell your story."

—*Vivian Gussin Paley*

Preparing to launch a family study in the classroom involves three inter-woven threads of activity: retrieving one's own memories of kin, becoming familiar with the wide range of literature and related materials on storytelling and family stories, and discovering how teachers in pioneering programs have developed successful family studies projects in their classrooms.

Before listening to the many writers, artists, and storytellers who work with children and teachers in New York City schools; before consulting folklorists, librarians, and oral historians; even before talking with colleagues about launching a family studies project, I turned to myself, to my own family stories. I looked through childhood photographs, asked an older relative to reminisce (and tape-recorded the reminiscence), and questioned whether my brother and my cousins had the same or different memories of growing up as I did. Then, as I began to draw on published guides[1] to collecting family stories, I tried out my ideas on myself and my family before the inspira-

---

[1] Please see the section entitled Resources for Teachers for references to these guides: Brown 1988; Davis 1993; Greene and Fulford 1993; Stone 1994; Zimmerman 1988.

tion slipped away. Ideally, I believe teachers should experience every aspect of family study themselves before introducing it to students.

Getting together with a small group of friends gave me the opportunity to share my family stories. There can be no better way to discover the power of family stories to connect people to themselves, to their families, and to one another than a period, however brief, of exchanging their own stories with others. Mary Savage, director of Henry Street Settlement's Parent Storytelling Workshops, says, "If you give a story from your heart, then others give stories in return. This way a community of shared literature and mutual understanding grows up where, before, there may have been unfamiliarity, tension and suspicion" (1993:2). Mary Helen Washington's anthology *Memory of Kin* grew out of a discussion group at her church. "For weeks," she says, "we read, analyzed, discussed and argued over the meanings of the stories that black writers told about family and what those stories helped to reveal to us about our own families and our place within them" (1991:vii).

FAMILY STUDY AT MANHATTAN COUNTRY SCHOOL

Family Study, a pioneering program at Manhattan Country School, began in 1981 with an idea of then–assistant teacher Laura Daigen. She convinced Augustus Trowbridge, the school's founder and director, that the social studies program of a school committed to diversity should reflect the racial, cultural, and socioeconomic diversity among the faculty, staff, and pupils. As a first step toward this end, Daigen proposed that the children study themselves—what they liked to eat, games they liked to play, what they did on weekends, when they went to bed. She also suggested that the children include the childhoods of their parents and grandparents.

"As developed by four successive head teachers," says Trowbridge (1993), "the Family Study curriculum has proved the depth of its inspiration by its immense flexibility. The idea of blending research with a sense of community has sparked a wealth of teaching plans made powerful as the children's natural interest in themselves and their budding curiosity about each other spur them to a new level of thinking."

Each year, early in October, the seven-eights, as second graders are known at MCS, take home a letter from their teachers that briefly outlines the Family Study curriculum. A meeting soon follows, on parent night, at which parents, teachers, and other family members come together to discuss the details of the project and its potential impact on each family.

Families whose children have been at MCS for some years are already familiar with related projects, beginning with home visits to the four- and five-year-old group. The following year, a small stuffed animal goes home with each five- and six-year-old and the "animal" writes letters, shared in class, about each family. Even with such preparation starting the family project with an open discussion is crucial to its success because the assignment to work on family stories tends to evoke powerful, even explosive, feelings in adults, as Krogness (1987) discovered in studying family folklore with her sixth graders in Shaker Heights, Ohio.

Before the first parent meeting takes place, a letter about Family Study is sent home to the parents (see Fig. 1-1). Once parents are involved, it's time to focus on the children. Children, like the rest of us, become more genuinely

Dear 7-8's parents,

Beginning tomorrow, your child will be researching family history by interviewing one of you. The children have spent the last two weeks creating questions and categories, and choosing questions they think are interesting, to ask you.

The interviews are due back on January 24th.
Your child will be asking you a total of 16 questions, so you and s/he will need to plan time for the project. The interview comes with some suggestions, but feel free to make your own.

As usual, we have encouraged the 7-8's to write down answers as they hear them; if your child has questions about spelling, it's fine to help.

We appreciate your time and help with this project in advance, and hope you enjoy it.

See you soon,

Valerie, Krina, and Stephanie

FIG. 1-1: Letter to Parents

interested in listening to stories from others if they are first given a chance to tell stories about themselves. MCS teachers begin Family Study by telling the children, *"You* are an important part of your family," and asking, "What do you look like?" Children are invited to make self-portraits and, later, masks of their faces (see Fig. 1-2). Krina Patel, who helped develop this maskmaking project, emphasizes that facial masks are not intended to be replicas of the children's faces, but are rather "an exploration of their characteristics through art, a dramatized version of their faces." Painstaking self-observation, corroborated by classmates, with special attention to skin color, facial structure, hair texture, and the like, results in remarkably accurate self-portraits.

The self-portraits and masks are clearly linked, in the children's perceptions, to personal identity and to family. One child was overheard saying to a classmate, "No, no, that looks more like my mom's color. I'm lighter than that." Another, pleased with his mask, said proudly, "We can pass them on. We can show the masks to our children. We can teach them how to make masks."

Valerie Gutwirth (1997) has described the mask project in detail, including the process of making masks. A simplified version utilizes the following steps:

1. With the teacher's help, the children cut out a basic oval shape from a nine-by-twelve-inch piece of oak tag, saving the cut-off edges to use for ears and noses. Next, they make a two-inch cut at the top, bottom, and sides of the oval. Finally, they overlap the slit edges and staple them together.
2. They paint their ovals in skin colors, using tempera poster paints in primary colors, adding dabs of black and white as needed, consulting with each other instead of using mirrors until they have obtained the best approximation of their own skin tones. They help each other decide on eye color as well, using colored Cray Pas and colored pencils. (The masks can be made more substantial by applying papier mache to the oak tag before painting.)
3. For eyebrows and hair, the children cut out scraps of colored paper and glue them onto the facial masks. When the masks are completed, they are put on display around a map of the world, with strings linking them to countries where the children's ancestors originated.

Another early Family Study activity is a brainstorming session in which each child chooses one question to ask the others: for example, "When is your bedtime?" This activity sets the tone for the duration of the project: We are not only learning about our own families, but also about others and their

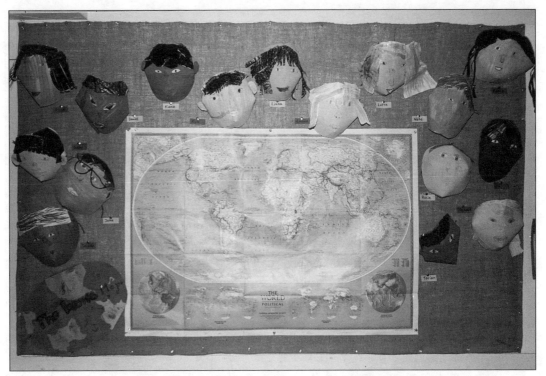

FIG. 1-2: Facial Masks on Display Around a Map of the World

families. "Every year is different," says Gutwirth, "in terms of the questions used and the amount of sharing with peers."

Learning about families can take many forms. When linking family information to the math curriculum, for example, the teacher helps the children construct graphs showing the range of variation in answers to questions about children's preferences in sports, foods, and the like. "First, we made up questions," one child explains, "then we got the answers and made a sloppy copy of our bar graphs. The final copy was in color."

The children also learn about the origin of their names and sometimes the names of relatives. A child describes the process: "We found out who named us and why they chose our names. Then we wrote about it and made a drawing with it. When they were all finished, we put them together in a book. We kept the book in class so everyone could read each other's stories." Sharing such illustrated pieces extends children's knowledge of their own and others' families and family traditions (see Fig. 1-3).

A time before I was born,
Mom and Dad wanted a strong
name for me. Mom wanted
Christopher, but Dad said, "No.
Let's call him Timothy." Grandma
Broome wanted a saint's name, so
Augustine became my middle
name. That was great because it is
part of my dad and brother's
middle name, Augustus. Now we
three have middle names that
start with "A."

FIG. 1-3: Timothy's Name Story

Elizabeth Simons (1990) tells us how she uses her own name to introduce this aspect of family folklore. "I tell the students that names are important," she writes, "that they not only define us, they also contain our family histories. Interviewing someone about her name will reveal her family-naming folklore and her family as well. As I write all of my names, past and present—ELIZABETH JANE RADIN SIMONS—on the board, I challenge the class, 'Try and find out as much as you can about me by asking questions about my name.'"

During the early stages of Family Study, the children write short, reflective pieces about family holidays like Thanksgiving or about birthday celebrations and related traditions. They also begin to collect information about family keepsakes and heirlooms, then write and illustrate pieces about them.

Working first with paper and later with fabric, the children make a class quilt representing all these objects. The paper quilts consist of four squares made by each child, with illustrations of family treasures. All the paper quilts, with their accompanying illustrated stories, are bound into a book. The fabric quilt, completed toward the end of the Family Study, includes one patch for each child, sewn with an applique; all the patches are stitched together. The children's descriptions of the squares they make for the fabric quilt show how much thought goes into the choice of each object. One child chose a mirror that had belonged to a grandfather she never knew. Another chose a ball: "It is important to my dad. He likes it because he caught it." Another decided to include a carrot: "It is Larry's. Larry is my mother's boyfriend. A carrot is on this square because he complains if my mom does not buy some from the store. He eats them very often."

The symbolism of the quilt project is not lost on the seven-eights: "The reason why we are making a quilt is that we are being sewn together," said one. "The piece that says 'seven-eights' is in the middle," another pointed out. "It's like the North Star and all the other pieces lead to the North Star because we're all connected, because we're in the seven-eights."

Children sometimes make collages to represent their families. Working with half the class at a time, the teacher demonstrates how to make a first draft on newsprint. One child plans to use a photo of a red toy car to symbolize her brother, playing cards for her dad, a drawing of a radio with musical notes bubbling out of it for her sister, and a book for her mom. A classmate pastes a map of the world onto construction paper; he plans to pinpoint the countries of origin and the present locations of family members on it. He chooses a photograph of himself to symbolize his grandma "because I'm her favorite hobby." Opposite him another boy is making several drawings: In one, his dad is cooking; in others his grandpa is making a sculpture and his mom is working at a computer. The gathering of symbolic objects and pictures generates a tangible presence of each child's family so that the classroom seems to be filled with the children's relatives. Later, the children will add written comments to the collages, indicating why they chose certain symbols and what each one represents about a family member.

Throughout the first months of Family Study, during morning meetings of the whole class, the children constantly discuss and revise their answers to questions such as "What is a family?" and "Who is in your family?"

What is a family? What do all families share?
by the seven-eights

A group of people that share a home together and food.

People who love each other.

People who care about each other and listen to what each other say.

People who share a room with each other and other things.

People who get married and might have kids and raise them.

A group of people who are related.

People who share toys.

A family is something that keeps going on and on.

The family keeps getting shorter and getting bigger because
people die and children are born.

It's like telling a story over and over again.

Junius Harris, who taught the Family Studies curriculum for several years, reminds us that, "because of how families have evolved over the last twenty years, there are many interpretations of a 'family.' A 'family' is not going to be just like your family or the one on the TV commercial, but there will be similarities that make the definition valid." To help define "family" in discussions with the seven-eights group, teachers read aloud from a selection of picture books that present pertinent family information. For example, the class learns the concept of generations through Lucille Clifton's book *The Lucky Stone*.[2]

For those teachers who might wonder what to say when children ask questions about their own family, this is what Gutwirth suggests: "When children ask about a teacher's family, it's best to answer only as much as necessary. You can say where you grew up and how many sisters and brothers you have, but this is not a study about the teacher's family and I don't want them thinking they have to tell a story that's the same as mine. I give examples, at the beginning of our discussions, when the kids are sometimes caught in stereotypes. I might say that my parents are divorced and don't live together. This gets them started. Once they see what's possible, they go right off and then the examples come from the children."

In the course of discussion, children learn that a family can be defined to include only members of their household; or all of their blood relatives,

---

[2] Other books that relate to this and other parts of the curriculum are presented by category in the annotated bibliography at the end of this book.

wherever they might live; or even, as some children insist, unrelated people they always depend on, like their babysitter, who calls for them every day when school's over.

After arriving at their definitions, the children are ready to study their families in greater depth and they work to convey what they learn to each other. As they move into the next phase of Family Study, the seven-eights begin to think about how their lives are like and unlike the lives of not only their classmates but also their parents and grandparents as well.

2

Then and Now

*Far into the future, your family will read your words
or listen to your voice and be grateful you took the time
to put this gift together for them.*

—Greene and Fulford

Involving grandparents or other elders is a particularly rewarding part of the Family Study at MCS. It has always included an exchange of letters. This activity prepares the children, to some extent, for tackling the parent interviews that come next by teaching them how to develop good questions for their letters to grandparents. In brainstorming discussions with teacher and classmates, each child develops a list of questions to include in the grandparent letter. Often grandparents reply with long and entertaining stories and express their joy at having an occasion to write them down for their families. Their eagerly awaited responses are read aloud in class.

Toward the end of October, seven-year-old Gina wrote a letter to her grandpa in Florida, asking him to tell her what life was like when he was a child (see Fig. 2-1). In early November, Gina's grandpa wrote back (see Fig. 2-2).

When Gina's teacher asked the class to write what they had learned from grandparents' letters in their own words, Gina wrote, "He made a lot of noise and had to move. He had four brothers and one sister. Italian and Jewish people live(d) in his neighborhood."

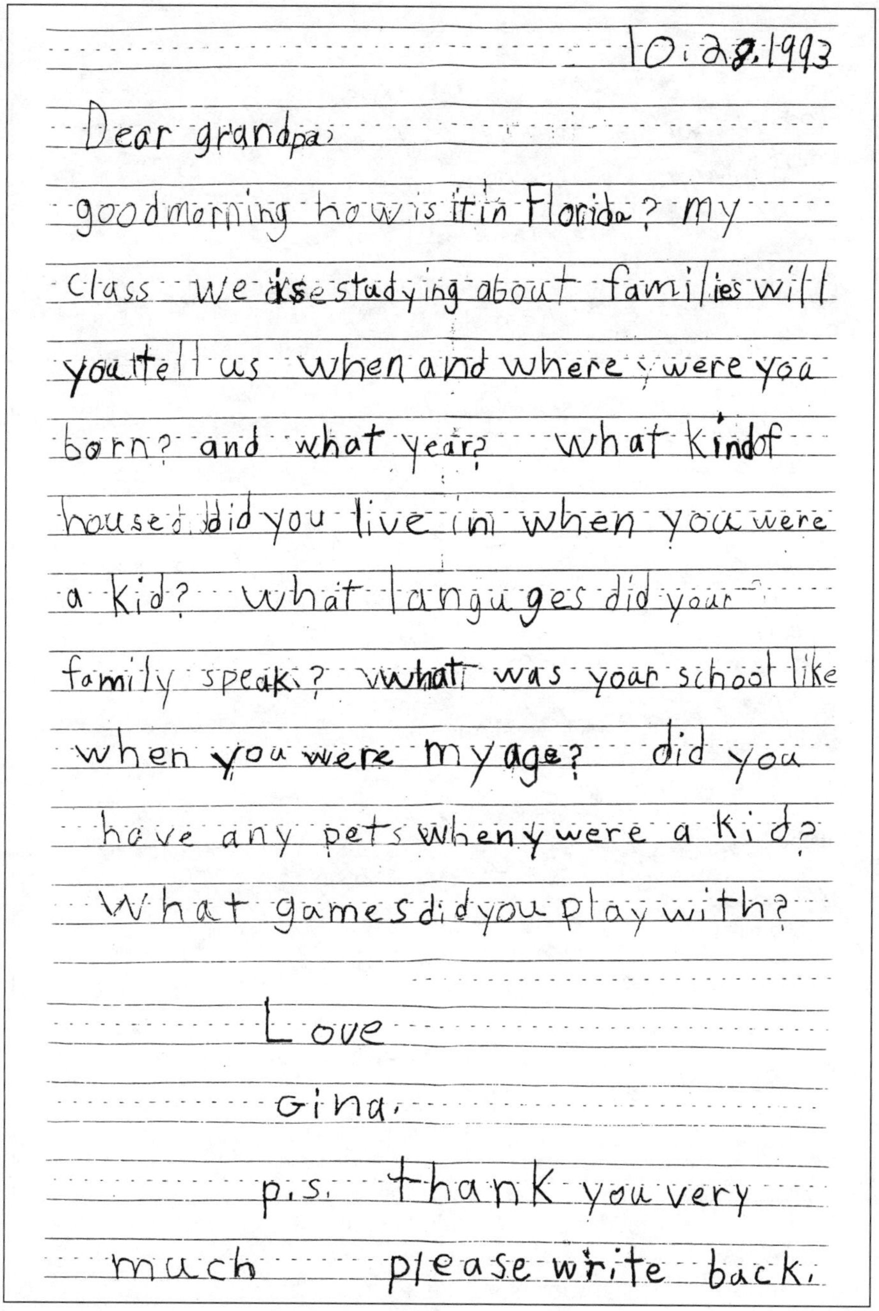

10.28.1993

Dear grandpa,

goodmorning how is it in Florida? my class we is studying about families will you tell us when and where were you born? and what year? what kind of house did you live in when you were a kid? what languges did your family speak? what was your school like when you were my age? did you have any pets when y were a kid? What games did you play with?

Love

Gina.

p.s. thank you very much please write back.

FIG. 2-1: Gina's Letter to Her Grandpa

We were six children close in age. As kids we were so busy fighting with each other, there was no time to play with toys - or to have pets - No animal had enough ~~to~~ tolerance To ~~stand~~ stay with us. In fact we made so much NOISE that the Landlord (the owner of the house) asked us or rather compell us to leave. It was very difficult to ~~~~ find a landlord who would accept a family with six ~~and~~ brotty kids.

My parents decided enough is enough, decided to find a home to buy. They bought a house a small one but neat, it had a backyard. A porch ~~areas~~ where we could play, It was located in Boro Park, a section of Brooklyn. We lived on a block that consisted of Italian and Jewish families. As children we got along amiably. ~~~~ Rarely early was any hostility.

As youngsters we played many games - Hide and Seek, Johnny on the pony, ski-the cat (asked Daddy or monny to explain) , base ball, Languages that were - Jewish and English; my mother spoke to us in Jewish and we responded in English

I hope this response pleases you,
        ALL MY LOVE   GRANDPA

FIG. 2-2: Part of Grandpa's Response to Gina

Mapping the locations of grandparents, their countries of origin, or the routes they took to reach the United States poses a challenge for seven- and eight-year-olds, who need concrete approaches to what is inherently an abstract concept. Teachers connect the children to maps in an organic way. First, they familiarize themselves with the concept of a map by handling wooden jigsaw puzzle pieces that represent states or countries. Next, they make maps of their own imagined places, using oak tag and construction paper for land masses; with colored markers they add winding, wavy lines for rivers and mountains, and straight lines for the borders between countries or states.

After completing the grandparent letters and maps, the children turn to their next assignment: learning to interview a parent or other significant adult in order to write an adult biography.

LEARNING TO INTERVIEW

Sometimes MCS teachers model the interview procedure in class with one of their own adult family members acting as interviewee. Children respond by talking about what makes for a good interview and by interviewing each other in pairs. Sometimes they make tape recordings of the process and listen to discover what kinds of questions brought the fullest answers.

A writer who has been going into New York City public schools for several years as an oral historian recently described two of her most innovative techniques for launching children on family interviews (McEwen 1995:136–143). She calls the first "The Silent Interview," and the second "Mrs. Rainey's Grandma."

The Silent Interview

"On the very first day," says McEwen, "before anything, before 'listening skills' and 'closed and open questions' and all the other jargon of the trade, I talk to the children about what I call the 'silent interview.' I stand in front of them, up by the board, and I ask them one question: What do you know about me without even asking?" The children reply that she is a woman; they guess at her age, height, weight, and, because she has an English accent, they also guess that she may come from England, Ireland, or Australia. The writer thus uses herself as a subject for this first, silent interview. It gives her a sense of how open, observant, and responsive the children are.

The Oral History Interview

Knowing that a classroom teacher who deals with children day after day may not want them to know too much about her, McEwen has invented an innovative exercise in which teachers can preserve their privacy and still present themselves as the subjects for an oral history interview. It calls for the class to interview their teacher, known here by the generic name "Mrs. Rainey," not as herself but in the character of her grandmother.

Some teachers may feel uneasy about embarking on this project. Do they have to answer every single question? No. McEwen tells them, "If you don't want to answer something you just say so. 'I don't want to answer that.' Or, 'No comment.'"

McEwen suggests a little homework for teachers who are planning to try "Mrs. Rainey's Grandma." She asks them to take a look at some old photographs, talk to a brother, a sister, or a great aunt. "See if you can remember the way your grandmother used to stand, the clothes she liked to wear—her favorite clothes, not her best ones. What were her friends like? What sorts of things gave her pleasure? Was she a gardener, a churchgoer; did she like to travel?"

On the day of the interview, the classroom teacher has already decided what age to be when taking on the role of "Mrs. Rainey's Grandma." Before McEwen introduces "Grandma" to the class, she talks to the children "as if they were a group of aspiring journalists." She tells them what she knows about the visitor, writing on the board her name, age, and the city and country in which she was born. Usually, she pulls out a big map of the world and asks the children to help locate those places. Next, she encourages the class to think up some specific questions that will help them discover more about the mystery visitor: "How many brothers and sisters does she have? What did her father do? Her mother? Did she go to school when she was little? If so, what were her favorite subjects?"

At this point, McEwen talks about interview technique, mentioning the difference between "closed" and "open" questions. Sometimes children give examples of the difference, showing that closed questions have only one answer, such as "Yes" or "No," while open questions bring longer, fuller answers. For example, "Did you play hopscotch when you were little?" is a closed question while "What kinds of games did you play when you were a kid?" is an open question. McEwen also discusses follow-up questions: What might they want to ask next if the interviewee tells them, for example, that she has eight brothers and sisters?

Before the visitor arrives, the children write down four questions to ask her. They can be new questions, or they can be some of the questions the class listed earlier. But they must be polite questions. And the children must remember to speak slowly and clearly and not interrupt each other. "We really need her to hear everything we're saying."

Then, with as much flair as she can muster, McEwen introduces the class to the interviewee, asks for a round of applause to welcome her, "and the children, somewhat startled, start to clap." Pointing again to the few words she has written on the blackboard, McEwen invites the children to fire their questions.

The visitor takes all the questions in stride. McEwen writes all her answers on the board, not making a big deal of it, not even writing complete sentences. But the information remains up there and the spelling is there in case it is needed later when the children write up the interview.

"Meanwhile," McEwen writes, "some of the children are baffled." They point out that the visitor is actually their classroom teacher. "Yes," I tell them, "but today she is pretending to be her grandmother." They go on with the interview.

At some point the children begin to realize that the interviewee is a direct line to information about their teacher. "Oh, she's your granddaughter! Is she your favorite? What was she like as a child? What year was she born? Was she ever really bad?" In most cases such questions can be easily handled. McEwen reminds the children that the visitor doesn't have to answer everything they ask her. "Please remember that she is an old lady, and that her memory isn't always so good any more." Teachers vary in how much they are comfortable revealing. Some will try to answer everything. "The kids appreciate such honesty enormously," McEwen writes. She tells us, "I will always remember the teacher who answered 'Not exactly,' when the children asked her if her grandmother was married. It was a wonderful moment, and I think it was terrifically reassuring to the kids, many of whom came from single-parent families."

When the interview is over and the visitor has been ushered out with applause, McEwen asks the children to write something about Mrs. O'Donnell, as "Mrs. Rainey's Grandma" is called here. They can write anything at all, anything they remember. (And the spelling is there on the board, just in case.) Afterward, three or four children read aloud what they have written, and the session on interviewing is over.

The crucial thing for teachers, in deciding whether or not to try "Mrs. Rainey's Grandma," McEwen reminds us, is what teachers know about themselves. Are they proud of their heritages, glad for the chance to tell their stories? Are they flexible? Do they know how to laugh? Can they draw boundaries when they need to and say "I'm sorry, but I can't answer that?" Only the teacher, herself, can know all these things, and she needs to find them out before taking on an exercise like "Mrs. Rainey's Grandma" so that the children's first experience in interviewing is as joyful and stimulating as possible.

At Manhattan Country School, the children hone their interviewing skills by developing a list of questions in brainstorming sessions and interviewing a classmate. On the basis of this experience, they create a more detailed list for their adult interviews. A letter describing the project, with suggestions for how parents might help children organize time for completing it, goes home with the questionnaire itself (see Fig. 2-3). Children receive instructions for planning the time needed to complete their interviews.

The adult biography that stems from the interview is a good way to enlarge the children's perceptions of adults as individual people. At first, children present the interview results orally and respond to comments and questions from classmates. Learning to ask questions that elicit interesting information is one of the areas of greatest growth in Family Studies. The children begin by asking such questions as What is your favorite color? or Did you like to skate? They discover, by trial and error, how much more they can learn with broader questions such as What did you play? and What did you like to eat? When the written biographies are completed and shared, unexpected stories and revelations get the whole class excited.

Children sometimes organize Family Museums, displaying artifacts that represent answers to some of the questions from the adult interviews. A desk nameplate from mother's office, for example, not only indicates that she works but may also provide information about her profession such as the initials R.N. or M.D. after her name. A father's, uncle's, or aunt's army dog tags have the owner's name, age, rank and religious affiliation inscribed on them and provide a memorable artifact from that person's past.

The concluding step in this interview process is to write an illustrated biography. From interview to final draft of the biography, a child develops many skills and, equally important, has special opportunities to sort things out in his or her own life. For example, an adopted boy wrote his mother's biography in great detail, checking every fact with his grandparents; he also wrote a piece about his birth mother. For a child who is being raised by a grandparent, the interview and biography can be done with the grandparent, and the earlier exchange of letters can take place between the child and another grandparent, or an aunt or uncle, or another relative or friend.

At several points during the Family Study, the children assess their progress to see how much they have accomplished and to tie together the various parts of the project. Recently, a teacher overheard a child in the seven-eights group describing the Family Study curriculum to a younger

{Parent Interview}

name _____

{Instructions}

Over the next eleven (11) days you will interview a parent.
Read this with your parent <u>before</u> you begin !

The interview has 16 questions, marked with an **X** in the box.
You will need to plan time to do the interview.
{DO NOT DO IT ALL AT ONCE.}

Here are three (3) possible plans:

<u>Plan A</u> : One question each weeknight, 2 or 3 each weekend day.

<u>Plan B</u>: Four questions each weekend day.

<u>Plan C</u>: One category every day or every other day.

Write your parent's answers down carefully.
Ask for help if you need it.

{Bring the finished interview back on Monday, January 24th}

G☺☺D LUCK !!

FIG. 2-3: Parent Interview Instructions

Dan's favorite board game was Monoply. Dan's favorite, outside game was base ball. Dan like To do side walk surfing on his skate boord. Dan walked to a hill on The streeT with his skate boord. Dan's best friend was Ira. Dan collecTed base ball cards of his favoriTe players. and he traded with his friends.

Dan had a radio and a T.v.. He goT To waTch an hour a day and he could lisTen To The radio as long as he wanTed Too. The name of his School was corn well avenue school and he walk There. Dan's mom helped his school. I Think Dan's school was fun because he

FIG. 2-4: Adult Biography

schoolmate from the six-sevens class: "In the fall you think, 'This is impossible. I'll never be able to do it.' By the end you think, 'This is easy and short.'"

At the culmination of the project, the children give a family party, usually a potluck dinner. At this time they share the process and the results of their work, and each child reads aloud from his or her adult biography or family story (see Fig. 2-4). The pride the children feel in themselves and in their fam-

had so many friends in school. Dan

Traveled by car or by walking. Cars got

smaller and faster and Dan got bigger

and slower. Gum cost 10¢ Toy cost

5$ movies cost $1.50 when Dan was little

gum I Think costs $1.50 Toy can

cost up t $10000 now.

InTerviewing My dad was fun. I liked it

because it took a short Time To finish, and

because I liked To learn about his

Childhood.

P.S. The End!!!!!!!!

FIG. 2-4: Adult Biography (continued)

ilies is evident as they read to an audience fascinated by their accounts. One child described the maskmaking project in this way: "None of the masks are the same. We all have different skin colors. We asked our classmates to be mirrors for us. I used mostly one brown crayon, and it took a long time." Displaying his Family Tree diagram, another child remarked, "We found out that we have much more people than we thought in our families." And the audience responded with appreciative laughter when one youngster read aloud from her adult biography, "Far, far away in New Britain, Connecticut, there lived a girl whose name was Susan. She loved reading Nancy Drew books. She looked like this: skinny, glasses, straight brown hair. Her husband didn't know this."

Parents, for their part, learn more about other families in the school and delight in seeing how their children have become valued members of an accomplished group. They also make discoveries about how they are perceived by their children, as evidenced by remarks made during the celebration." Some of the things I thought were important about my childhood were unimportant to my child," says one parent. A father, who used the adult biography interviews to let his child know that he had been married to another woman before marrying her mother, agrees: "That bit of information is not in the biography, but the hamster I had as a kid is in there." And a mother reported that she had participated in the Family Study three times without losing interest. "Each of my children took a different aspect of my life as the main focus of their interviews. One was interested in travel; the second wanted to know about all the summer and part-time jobs I had while I was in school; the third focused on my interest in art."

When the seven-eights move on to their next project—a study of mammals—they bring with them solid skills developed in the Family Study, which they can apply to book research. They have learned to gather and reflect on many facts, to ask interesting questions, to translate information into many forms for others' enjoyment, and to understand some of the similarities and differences between their own and others' families.

FAMILY STUDY: AN EVOLVING CURRICULUM

Family Study continues to evolve at Manhattan Country School. Issues involving gender equity, adoption, single parent households, and families headed by gay or lesbian parents are some of the topics currently under discussion. Some MCS middle school students and their teacher recently participated in *It's Elementary*, a documentary film in which children and teachers discuss gay and lesbian issues in various schools around the United States. This topic is increasingly receiving attention from primary school educators, as evidenced by articles in journals (Casper, Schultz and Wickens 1992; Wickens 1993). Perhaps most important of all, the children themselves have begun to speak. At P.S. 87, a New York school that is also featured in *It's Elementary*, one child submitted an essay about her two moms to a community-sponsored Mother's Day writing contest in which she won first prize (see Fig. 2-5).

Although haveing two mothers is a promblem to others I respect that that's the way they think and I can't do eny thing about it. [I still think that thoose people think stupidly.] This once happend with a boy in my class who could not come to my house because my parents were lesbian. One night I called their house and the mother told me their versian off the bible. I stood up for my mothers and new that many kids of my class were suporting me and calling me to see how I was. I am prod of my moms and enioy marching in the gay pride march every single year with my moms.

Emily Beth Maryann
PRIDE PRIDE MOMS PRIDE

FIG. 2-5: My Two Moms

Counterparts of the MCS Family Study have also been implemented in public schools. Laura Daigen, who helped initiate it at MCS, was one of the first to use the Family Study curriculum successfully in this other setting. "Students listened intently to each other during our discussion," she reports. "They seemed very interested in hearing what everyone else's families were like. I think they wanted to know they weren't alone." She and others teaching in public schools have found that the family structures of their pupils tend to be more complex than those of most children at MCS. Either parent's presence in the household cannot be taken for granted. Children may participate in a pattern of moving among several households, living with grandparents and other relatives and also, at times, with godparents and family friends who act as kin. In response to these patterns, teachers find it useful to shift the major focus of class discussions to households and their composition, learning about the range of adults who play a care-giving role in the children's lives.

Other public school teachers in the New York metropolitan area who have either taught at MCS or participated in its weekend training workshops have found that public school students welcome an opportunity to learn about their own and their classmates' families, especially those that reflect a wide racial, cultural, and economic diversity. Nicole Elliott, who teaches a racially and economically mixed group of fourth graders in New Jersey, says the children are very aware of the differences among them. "It overshadows anything else we might do. There is no common footing, very little similarity in experience among them. Some are more physically aware or more in touch with the world than others. Some speak casually of brothers and sisters in the criminal justice system. Several of them live in foster care families."

To defuse any tension and help them understand each other's lives, Elliott draws on the children's familiarity with family life as portrayed on television, asking them to compare characteristics of situation-comedy families that reflect stereotypes of race and/or economic status. In addition, she asks her class to hold a family breakfast in the spring as the culmination of the unit on immigration. A parent presides at each cooking station; food is prepared in electric frying pans and on hot plates. Each group of children, together with a parent, is considered a family. Each family observes relevant dietary restrictions, if any, and the children discuss the contexts in which such restrictions are observed. But, even though the breakfast is popular, Elliott finds the focus on variations in food limiting. Thus she is seeking ways to study families in greater depth, with the aim of eventually encouraging her students to explore relevant issues of social justice.

3

News from the Home Front

Every night now, I tell stories to my children after the books have been put away and the lights are off. I have no choice; they beg me for them. After I'm done, they tell their own. Already they are becoming links in the chain.

—*Pamela Crimmins, Parent Coordinator*
Family Storytelling Project, Children's Workshop School

There is a growing body of evidence that personal storytelling is an area of strength for many preschoolers, including those from low income and minority backgrounds (Heath 1983). Stories of personal experience, told by people in the course of ordinary, everyday life, have significance for children as moral tales, models of exemplary lives, humor, and social commentary (Zeitlin, Kotkin and Baker 1982). They also expose children to a variety of narrative practices and give them tools to express and make sense of who they are (Miller and Mehler 1994).

Approaches to the teaching of reading and writing that build upon children's oral skills and experience in relating personal stories (Calkins 1982; Michaels 1981; Rosen 1988) recognize that personal storytelling provides a basis for early literacy and a good bridge between the worlds of home and school.

Vascellaro and Genishi (1994) have shown what an impact the sharing of personal stories can have on teachers' lives and on their practices. But what are the implications of opening these classroom practices to include the children's families in personal storytelling? What happens when teachers invite families into the classroom to tell personal stories? These questions are addressed from the perspectives of several teachers and families whose experiences are presented in this chapter.

FAMILY STORYTELLING IN KINDERGARTEN

In the early 1990s, Cornell University's Cooperative Extension Service began workshops in several New York City school districts for parents and teachers who wanted to tell family stories in their children's classrooms. Cheryl Tyler, who teaches kindergarten at P.S. 75, became an enthusiastic participant who then incorporated family storytellers in her own classroom. "One of the first things we learned was that a story for children needs a positive outlook," she says. "None of those 'When I was a kid, I had it hard' kinds of stories."

Cornell's trainers also emphasized the importance of making both parents and teachers feel comfortable about how they might choose to participate. Sometimes people "may be shy, or they may be working fourteen hours a day," Tyler explains. "Some feel their family is not very interesting; others may lack fluency in English. Those without permanent residency cards feel disenfranchised and they're frightened to speak." Tyler confirms, however, that those who do participate, even if only by coming and listening to other storytellers, strengthen their sense of connection with the school. Eventually, many are ready to try telling stories themselves.

At first, the focus is on where the storytellers grew up and on the stories and traditions that have been passed on to them by their families. Tyler begins by telling stories of her own childhood. Next, she invites her own parents to come and tell about theirs. Soon, the kindergarten children's families are ready to participate. One mother told stories about her father growing up in Turkey, tales of transcending loneliness and learning to take responsibility. A Jewish parent showed a film about preparing foods for a traditional holiday meal. A Muslim parent dressed her child in traditional clothing when she came in to tell stories. Another parent, who had grown up in Egypt, told a silly story about tossing mud balls at her family's white house; then she told a sad story about the time she threw her beloved doll into the Nile river as a personal reenactment of an ancient ritual in which sacrifices were made to end droughts. Her son gave her such a sad look, she said, that "he seemed to be saying, "Don't worry, Mommy, I'll be your doll." One of the children's favorite tales was a real knee slapper about a father's great-great-grandfather's mail-order false teeth and the ornery billy goat who got hold of them.

The children respond to these stories, making them their own, by drawing pictures of the characters or settings in their journals, sometimes with explanatory captions, or by painting posters to illustrate their favorite scenes. Tyler sets up a storyteller's tent so that small groups of children can listen to parents telling stories without disturbing others. A reporter from the *New York Times* came to listen; he informed his readers that the stories he heard in Ms. Tyler's kindergarten class "proclaimed the city's human mosaic" (Martin 1991). The children were attentive to all the stories; however, when storytellers talked for a longer time than Tyler felt was appropriate, she used a prearranged signal to let them know it was time to stop.

For the second year of the storytelling project, Tyler received a grant from the school district and purchased an oven. About half of the parents came in to cook special holiday dishes and tell the stories associated with them. Others did the cooking at home and brought the food to school. The children documented the cooking project with photographs and drawings and compiled the recipes in a class cookbook that was used to raise money for the parents association. The next year, in collaboration with New York City's Children's Museum, the kindergartners and their families organized their keepsakes and collections of trivia—everything from wartime army dog tags to baseball cards, bottle tops, and buttons—into a Family Museum, which they displayed in the classroom and then exhibited at the Children's Museum.

Tyler readily acknowledges the contribution of Cornell's storytelling workshops to the success of her family stories program. She recommends the following set of guidelines, developed by the workshop coordinators, for parents and teachers who wish to launch family stories projects in their schools:

- *Start at the top.* Anyone in the school can start the ball rolling, but the first step is to find someone to support you at or near the top. Often, the district superintendent or school principal is the person to contact at the outset. (Some teachers may prefer to start on their own, without engaging the larger school community.)
- *Go to the source.* Pull together a small group of people who are in a position to determine the district's or school's interest in the project and who will make sure it is properly implemented. Then arrange a visit by a storyteller/educator who has had experience in working with parents and teachers.
- *Build the teams.* Once a district/school has decided to implement the program, it is important to spread the word. Organize a family storytelling team of teaching and nonteaching staff, together with at least three parents, and spread the word.
- *Learn the ropes.* Some formal training of school teams is essential. Cornell suggests two half-day training sessions, typically held six weeks apart. All participants—teachers, parents, nonteaching staff, and administrators—are trained together. In the first session, parents and school personnel are introduced to the process of finding and sharing family stories of their own; each school then creates its own action plan for starting family storytelling. In the second session, the teams reunite with the trainers to review the progress made in preparing their schools for the project.

- *Make it stick.* Once the program is underway, and before summer vacation, it is important for each school to have in place a plan for the next year. Consider ways to involve more parents in family storytelling. Incorporate more school staff and people in the community. Making it stick often depends on making it fresh and new.
- *Keep it simple.* The process works best by starting small. Family storytelling is no place for razzle-dazzle or big ambitions. Keep the storytelling simple and sincere. It's the simple story with a heartfelt message that nurtures and connects all those who hear it.
- *How it works.* Family storytelling runs throughout the school year, usually on a weekly basis. Depending on the age of the children and the goals of the classroom teacher, the storytelling sessions last from twenty minutes to an hour at each visit.

In 1995, Tyler experimented with a new approach to family storytelling: a parent-child poetry project. "The playful, imaginative language of poetry is exactly the language we want the children to bring to all their writing," says Tyler. "And poetry has a special place at P.S. 75: Everyone knows the school is named for Emily Dickinson." From September until mid-December, Tyler drenched her students in poetry. As a class, they studied a new poem each week, listening to their teacher read the poems aloud, learning some by heart, and sharing them at home. There were poems everywhere in the room. Copied onto large sheets of newsprint or oak tag, they were hanging from a clothesline, clipped to an easel, and taped to the walls, windows, and closet doors. The children and the classroom were bursting with poetry. Poems spilled out into the corridor: "Twinkle, Twinkle, Little Star" hung on a wall just outside the door to K-124, adorned by a carefully lettered sign: Poem by Jane Taylor. With music by Mozart playing nearby, the poem was surrounded by the children's exuberant paintings of the night sky.

The day before winter vacation began, the children entertained their families at a poetry celebration in the classroom. Clapping, swaying, and nodding their heads to the rhythms of poems about insects and animals and colors—poems with syncopated call-and-response patterns like "Clap Your Hands, Keep On Clapping Them"—the children made the room reverberate with joyful sound as they sang, recited, and dramatized many of the poems they knew. "I always come to these events," one father told another. "I get behind in my work, but it's worth it." In closing, the children worked in pairs performing a catchy finger-snapping, handclapping routine as they recited Eloise Greenfield's "Things," a poem about making poetry. Responding to the rhythm, a few parents soon began snapping their fingers too.

The poet and teacher Georgia Heard (1989:1) tells us that when a teacher in one of her workshops recites a favorite poem learned in childhood, the others join in. Cheryl Tyler invited her kindergartners' parents to join in at the start of the new year. Then, early in January, Tyler wrote to the children's families, asking them to select favorite poems at home to share with their children and their children's classmates. "We will be compiling these poems in a class album," she wrote. "Take your time selecting your favorite."

Marie's mother was the first to respond. Her favorite poem was one by Robert Louis Stevenson. Having learned it as child, she memorized it. "I've never forgotten it because it meant a lot to me." She talked with Marie about how the poem expressed her confused, frustrated, almost painful feelings as a child, when she struggled to make sense of a grown-up rule about bedtime that seemed arbitrary and unfair in the long days of summer.

❖ ❖ ❖ ❖ ❖ ❖ ❖ ❖ ❖

Bed in Summer
Robert Louis Stevenson

In winter I get up at night,
And dress by yellow candle light.
In summer, quite the other way,
I have to go to bed by day.

I have to go to bed and see
The birds still hopping on the tree,
Or hear the grown-up people's feet
Still going past me in the street.

And does it not seem hard to you,
When all the sky is clear and blue,
And I should like so much to play,
To have to go to bed by day?

❖ ❖ ❖ ❖ ❖ ❖ ❖ ❖ ❖

Marie loved the poem as much as her mother did and soon knew it by heart. After her mom wrote it down, Marie brought the poem to school and proudly recited it to her classmates. Like a family heirloom, the poem was lovingly passed on to Marie by her mother; it was as precious as most keepsakes but considerably less fragile than some. Thus Marie carried her mother's favorite childhood poem to school in her pocket, with no fear of breaking or losing it.

Marie's mother commented that a kindergarten poetry project seemed quite sophisticated. She felt other parents might be slower to respond to Tyler's request for favorite poems than she had been. Characterizing herself as someone who escaped into books as a child and remained "constantly involved with words, playful with words" ever since, she was, indeed, more readily responsive to the poetry project than most other parents.

Inevitably, in a world in which even the most avid readers are not likely to spend time reading poetry, parents—to say nothing of teachers—are bound to find a poetry project for kindergartners sophisticated, maybe even intimidating. However, asking parents to share their favorite nursery rhymes tends to lessen anxieties and opens the assignment to siblings and other relatives as well.

In Tyler's class, for example, both Daniel's parents spent a great deal of time reading. They also frequently read aloud to their children, but they seldom read poetry. Searching for a poem in various poetry books and children's magazines to which the family subscribed did not help Daniel or his parents find one they liked enough to call a favorite. But when his older sibling produced a folder of poems collected during a first grade poetry study, Daniel found his favorite: "Fuzzy Wuzzy Was A Bear," a word play familiar to many English-speaking children and adults.

Fuzzy Wuzzy was a bear.
Fuzzy Wuzzy had no hair.
Fuzzy Wuzzy wasn't fuzzy
Wuzzy?

Daniel illustrated Fuzzy Wuzzy for the class collection; but at the culminating celebration, he hastily substituted a "second favorite" because he feared his classmates might laugh at him for choosing the "babyish" Fuzzy Wuzzy.

Unless parents and teachers validate the choice of "silly" or "babyish" verses and nursery rhymes, there is a risk that young children may renounce their favorites for the same reason Daniel did. Indeed, teachers and parents may also feel that teaching children's rhymes is silly and condescending. However, childhood verses can broaden the family stories project and provide a powerful way for teachers and parents to collaborate in leading children through the gateway to poetry. Moreover, poems of childhood, while they may vary in style and detail across different languages and cultures, can almost always be approximately translated from one language to another. This gives the genre an advantage in a classroom of children whose families represent diverse linguistic and cultural backgrounds. Translations made by adult relatives or by the children themselves can convey the spirit of the original in ways that will interest and entertain all readers and listeners.

Poems, rhymes, and ditties of childhood are the most familiar, the most colloquial forms of poetry we know. Lullabies; nursery rhymes; counting songs that use fingers and toes; calendar rhymes; limericks; verses about animals, flowers, good and bad children, and monsters—poems of childhood the world over have so many similarities that we can properly call them universal. Hearing or reciting them, adults reach back to their early emotional memory, down to the deepest part of themselves. Like family stories, childhood poems link the generations to come with those that have gone before.

COMMUNITY-BASED FAMILY STORYTELLING WORKSHOPS

Inviting families to share their favorite childhood rhymes, games, and songs is a good way to launch family storytelling projects. Mary Savage, a professional storyteller who directs the community-based Family Storytelling Workshops for the Henry Street Settlement in New York City, finds that they are good icebreakers. After sharing them with each other and with children in the classroom, some of the workshop families, under Savage's guidance, published a selection of their favorite songs and games.

Savage also draws on collections of folk and fairy tales in her workshops. Like songs, rhymes, and games, they are good sources because they come from traditional oral literature, are easy to learn, and usually bring to mind other childhood stories. She inspires listeners with tales from many different cultures and narrative traditions. If a visit from a professional storyteller like Savage is not practical, tape recordings made by storytellers at the National Storytelling Festival are good substitutes. Also, books on how to collect oral histories provide lists of stimulating questions that teachers like Savage have used to elicit family stories (e.g., Zeitlin, Kotkin and Baker 1982).

Listening respectfully is the key to getting others to share their living experiences through stories. With Savage as a model, parents at Children's Workshop School (CWS) began gathering family stories from all the adults in their school. One mother marveled, "It's incredible seeing people bring their kids to school every day, not knowing anything about them, and then hearing their stories. It's brought everyone together." Tape recording and transcribing parents' and teachers' stories made it clear that some people love to tell stories in any setting: at work, at lunch, on the phone, in their children's bedrooms, on car trips, in the classroom. But others feel no one would listen to them because what they've lived or what they know does not seem interesting or important. "Go ahead, let's hear it anyway," the story collectors at CWS would urge. They knew that a listener's genuine interest can usually persuade even reluctant storytellers to begin. Once they do, they discover that their lives are more interesting than they thought.

To keep the stories flowing, Savage (1996) suggests a number of strategies, such as asking the participants to draw a picture of where they grew up or a time line focused on a specific cultural topic—literacy, for example — across three generations of one's family. They then use these drawings as the basis for telling stories, working either in pairs or with the whole group. The mothers who attended Savage's storytelling sessions at the Children's Workshop School worked in pairs, using drawings of their childhood environments as springboards for sharing family stories with their partners. Each chose a topic to talk about for five minutes while the partner listened. "This was most helpful in focusing and choosing an appropriate story to tell in the classroom," one mother recalls. "You could begin to rule out certain subject matter, or you could phrase it in a way that made it acceptable and then start gearing your story for an audience of children."

After several weekly sessions, the parents were ready to apply the techniques they had learned, telling family stories in their children's classrooms, and tape recording the sessions so that others could learn from them. They also began gathering and tape recording stories from teachers, school staff, and other parents, ultimately publishing them in an anthology. In addition, they practiced telling simple tales, such as *The Three Little Pigs*, which they retold to increasingly large groups of children as they gained confidence in their storytelling skills. Pinpointing the beginning, middle, and end of a traditional tale introduced them to the strategy of structuring a story as a way to begin learning it by heart.

Learning a story by heart—not word for word—some tellers speak the story directly from their mental moving pictures. One mother at CWS made her own visual guideline, capturing and holding the attention of a kindergarten class with lively images that jogged her memories of her grandfather who was an inventor: how he grew up on a farm and went to a one-room schoolhouse; how he and his brothers and sisters made their own toys when they were children; how he drove a model-T Ford, worked as a grave digger to pay his way through college, and met his wife on a train; and he how created a pond on his own land, with an island and a bridge, making changes in it from year to year so that his grandchildren would always find something new and different there.

Alternatives to learning a story by visualizing the characters and sequence of action are simply to read it aloud repeatedly or tape it and listen to the recording until you know the words well. However, rather than breaking storytelling down into a step-by-step process, Savage relies on apprenticeship. Thus she never encourages people to learn from tapes or learn a story word for word since this may stunt a storyteller's style. This is an important point, she emphasizes, for working with families who tend to have a variety of educational backgrounds. It is also crucial for building a sense of community literature—a sense that, even if a story comes from a book or videotape, it finally resides in the storyteller and in his or her community.

When a story is ready for telling, children are the best beginning audience. At CWS, one parent recalls the time she and two other parents told stories in their children's classroom: "We were afraid of the children at first, but then we saw the response. All the kids remember us now, and they hug us when they see us in the hall." For these parents, telling stories has become "a way of living, a life skill" that connects them with children, other parents, and the adults in charge of the school.

Emphasizing that families are major sources of children's literacy (Taylor 1983), Savage's approach is influenced by the work of Paulo Freire (1973). She encourages participants to use their stories to transform their personal lives and the social worlds in which they live (1992, 1996), giving themselves a vision of a larger civic role than they may hitherto have played in their community or, rather, in the plurality of communities to which they belong for different purposes, at different times.

At P.S. 19, families have been participating in Savage's storytelling workshops for six years, meeting regularly at the school and at the Henry Street Settlement. Roaming through their memories and exchanging their personal stories, adults find that the workshops offer them a way of relaxing and letting go. One parent puts it this way: "Living in the city, you're uptight. Mary comes in and we relax, feel good. 'I shared something today'—that's how it makes you feel. I'd like to have a Mary in my house every day."

Parent-Child Storytelling Workshops

At one mother's suggestion, parent storytellers at P.S. 19 invited their fourth and fifth grade children to tell stories with them in the kindergarten classes. "Storytelling is more intense than reading aloud," one parent remarked. "The gestures, facial expressions, body movements—they all help shy children blossom." Her own daughter surprised her when they told Goldilocks together: "She put so much emotion into it. I'd go 'And the Papa Bear said,' and she'd take it from there. She's excited to come to it."

The atmosphere in the parent-child workshop is relaxed and informal. One mother brings a sleeping toddler in a stroller. Another holds an infant

Photographs of Family Storytellers

on her lap. A father stops by on his way to work and stays long enough for a cup of instant coffee. Several fourth graders are spending their lunch hour practicing storytelling with their families. Mary Savage begins the workshop with one of her favorite icebreakers: a story with a silly repetitive chant that usually charms even the most skeptical newcomers, "Mumbo-jumbo, Christopher Columbo, sitting on the sidewalk, eating bubble gumbo." Soon the fourth graders are chiming in.

At first, one fourth grader shows scant interest in storytelling. As the session continues, however, she becomes involved and reveals a gift for improvising, a good sense of timing, and a sense of humor: "Oh, no! The Big Bad Wolf's gonna eat us up! We'll be pork chops!" After she experiences the joy that comes from telling stories to responsive kindergarten children, she becomes an enthusiastic participant.

When the group enters a kindergarten classroom, the children are waiting, seated close together on a bright red rug in the sunny book corner. When introducing the storytellers to the audience, one of the parents praises the kindergartners, "You pay attention so well that today we have a special treat for you. We're going to tell you a story with two of the big girls from the

Photographs of Family Storytellers

fourth grade." A burst of spontaneous applause greets this announcement. Seated before them on child-sized chairs, the storytellers begin. A mother holding her two-year-old on her lap tells the group, "This is a story about three little pigs. Some of you know it already. But today, we're going to *tell* it to you, not read it." As soon as the story ends, the children ask for another. A second set of parents and children take over the storytellers' chairs. One parent sings "This Little Light of Mine" and, before long, many kindergartners are singing along.

    Parents who collaborate with their own and others' children in the storytelling workshop offer a wide range of comments: "Parent and child, working together on the same level: the kids love it." "Togetherness, a bond with children." "Storytelling is nurturing a lot of kids in this school who don't get enough of that." "I've been able to be more aware of what my kids feel." One young mother adds, "I'm giving my child's life into the teacher's hands. When a teacher knows my child's background, when parents in the school know where we come from, how we differ and what we have in common, it's happier for everyone." Another mother expresses her concern about what she calls the "flattening of our society." This happens, she feels, when a story like

"The Hunchback of Notre Dame" becomes a Disney cartoon. "Telling traditional stories ourselves is like reading aloud from the original texts. It counteracts this flattening effect and lifts us to another level."

PUBLISHING THE STORIES

"Made by Cerena Hernandez. For the People. This book was written January 1996." That's what it says, in English and in Spanish, on the last page of a little handmade book. Cerena's bilingual pop-up book, titled *My Bag/Mi Cartera*, documents and celebrates her participation in the parents storytelling workshop at P.S. 20. On its cover is a tiny replica of a woman's handbag made of pink construction paper, with a red dot for its fastener and a bit of white string for the handle. Shiny, pink, oval-shaped sequins sparkle at the scalloped edges of a red border that frames the title. Inside, on bright yellow paper, in Cerena's precise, delicate handwriting, are these words: "A Bag is important for women for keeping many important things, such as sentimental things, cosmetics, money, even First Aid." Leafing through the pages of Cerena's book, one discovers colorful examples of United States currency; lipstick and rouge containers; a small white Bible; and an accordion-pleated folder that holds photographs of Cerena's children, her parents, her husband, and herself. A glittery pink paper heart decorates the book's last page. "But my heart," writes Cerena, "is where I keep all my love for my children, my family, and for all the people in this world."

Like her bag, Cerena's original book holds "many important things," among them important implications for how such a book might be used effectively in different parts of the elementary curriculum. For example, in language arts, such a book fits nicely into minilessons on writing, reading, and speaking; in social studies, it suggests a unit on ethnic heritage (What's in your bag/knapsack/lunch box?) and a study of different historical periods; in mathematics, it encourages research on different kinds of currencies and practice in sorting, counting, adding, and subtracting; in the arts, it can be a springboard for oral storytelling, painting, drawing, collages, and more pop-up books. Whatever the subject, Cerena's book offers the humanizing, personalizing touch of family stories.

AFTER THE STORIES GO HOME

When stories are made into books, parents will read them to family members at home, at holiday gatherings, at birthdays, and when relatives come to visit. After the stories go home, and circulate through the family, and the community, some eventually return to school. A picture book version might be read aloud to a youngster at home before the child has learned to read; later, the same child might see a portion of the story displayed beside an enlarged photograph of the teller on a big poster in a community literacy festival; once the child learns to read the story on her own, she may proudly bring it back to school to show her teacher and her classmates. As their stories travel in complex circles from workshop to home and community, parents and children alike develop a first-hand sense of what it means to be an author. One story's journey from the Parent Storytelling Workshop to the teller's home and then back to school went like this: Delores Brown related how difficult was her ordeal in giving birth to her daughter Nickie. Tape recording her account, she transformed it into a book, which she took home with her.

"Nickie's Story" begins with her mother's memory of the night she was born. "All the snow this winter reminded me of the story of Nickie's birth. Nickie's story is always with me, but it's not a happy story. It was December 14, 1984. With my first child, with Tifa, giving birth was pretty good. I was new and I got a lot of needles and stuff, so I didn't have to think about a lot of pain. But with Nickie! Oh! The pain was so severe. It was so bad. And it was winter. I'll never give birth in winter again."

Part of the text was reproduced on a laminated poster, along with a photograph of Delores and Nickie. The poster was exhibited with several others at an annual community story fair. The full five-page story of Nickie's birth was printed in an anthology of parent-made literature published by Henry Street's Arts in Education program. By telling the story, making it into a book, and putting it out into the community, Nickie's mother was able to share a story that spoke to many others.

When Nickie learned to read the story herself, she took it to school. Word of "Nickie's Story" spread in school among her mother's acquaintances. (Excitedly waving the little book, a member of the school's support staff ran after a visitor in the corridor. "I've got this amazing book to show you," she said. "It's called 'Nickie's Story.'" "Oh, yes, I know," casually replied the visitor, who had heard the story some time ago in the parent storytelling workshop. "I'm friends with the author.")

CONTRASTS AND COMMONALITIES

The two approaches to family storytelling reviewed in this chapter differ in scope and their focus of activities. Cheryl Tyler's program is the more intimate and child-centered of the two; she is concerned exclusively with the children in her classroom and their families. Her emphasis is on how family storytelling supports the children's social, emotional, and academic development. Taking the lead, she sets the agenda for family stories in her kindergarten classroom. Parents respond by participating in whatever ways Tyler suggests, whether by sharing their special holiday dishes and the stories associated with them, creating exhibits of family trivia collections, telling stories and sharing keepsakes, or collaborating with their children on a poetry project. Each family participates in the classroom no more than a few times during the year, in ways that contribute to Tyler's curriculum goals. It is the children, not their families, who learn by heart the stories families tell and the poems they share. It is the children, with their teacher's help, who transform what they hear into text, making drawings of the stories and verses in their journals, creating a class cookbook of recipes contributed by families, and illustrating large posters used in classroom performances.

In contrast, Mary Savage coordinates a districtwide program that focuses primarily on adults, includes many schools, and engages the families of children from different classrooms within them. Working from a community base rather than in a single classroom, she adapts the participatory model of Paulo Freire, encouraging families to take the lead in developing the program, with the goal of helping them use their stories to begin transforming their lives and their communities. Participating families meet regularly with Savage throughout the year, exchanging stories with each other more frequently than they tell them in classrooms.

Perhaps because it is broader in scope, the community-based program seems more challenging than the one that is classroom based. Susan Fleminger, director of Henry Street Settlement's Arts in Education program, warns that family storytelling workshops are "not a quickie fix." Savage concurs: "Community-based work is different from school. In community settings, there's no signing up, no fee, and the ethic of going regularly to a workshop or class isn't common, even though the participants may do so in other parts of their lives. It takes time to convince people to call and reschedule when they can't attend." In addition, a workshop coordinator who arrives with the intention of teaching a new folktale or song, for example, must be prepared to have the goal of enlarging the parents' repertoire preempted by the parents' agenda. "We have our own issues," one mother emphasizes, "and sometimes we need to tell our own stories. They aren't all for kids."

The decision to use either of these approaches to family storytelling, or a combination of the two, will depend for the most part on the school and community situation in which a teacher is working. Whether classroom or community based, both projects emphasize the importance of a relaxed, modest approach in family storytelling. Both celebrate progress and closure, with performances in the classroom or at local libraries, banks, and bookstores. Both celebrate the stories and the tellers by disseminating family folklore generated in the program through publications, story museums, literacy fairs, and the like. Even more important are the common, underlying qualities of the individuals in charge. The teacher and the workshop coordinator demonstrate flexibility, patience, a sense of humor, and sensitivity to the needs and comfort of the participating families. All these, together with the continuing support of administrators, are required for a successful family storytelling project. The rewards are significant. Encouraging a view of parents as primary sources of children's literacy, family storytelling creates an extended classroom or school family; lessens the isolation of teachers, pupils, and parents; and, in an educational field that sometimes seems antiparent, increases optimism about developing effective family involvement in schools.

4

Stories to Grow Up On

*Each time a story is told about a child,
his place in the family is reaffirmed.*

—Deborah Shaw Lewis & Gregg Lewis

Kit Fung and Charlotte Norris have been teaching in New York City's public schools for more than twelve years. Working with contrasting groups of first graders under strikingly different conditions, they have developed distinct but complementary approaches—storytelling and memoir, respectively—that call forth stories from the intimate circles of home and family to the wider social world of school.

Through the examples they set, both teachers acknowledge and, indeed, honor the importance of relationships—parent-teacher-child-school—in literacy development. Through storytelling, Fung makes a gift of herself to the Chinese-American children she teaches by telling them stories her mother told her when she was a child. Inspired by Fung's example, several of her colleagues and, eventually, some of the children's parents and grandparents also share their family stories with the children. In like manner, Charlotte Norris creates, through the use of memoir, a classroom atmosphere of social happiness, awareness, and cohesion in which children feel safe enough to reveal themselves to her and to each other. She leads her first graders toward an understanding of what kinds of subjects are suitable for a memoir, in part by showing them some of her personal treasures, the souvenirs and mementos she cherishes because they remind her of important people and events in her life. What is equally significant, Norris also engages parents in helping their children remember experiences that are vivid and meaningful enough to provide a basis for the making of memoir.

STORYTELLING AT P.S. 124

At P.S. 124, the children come mainly, though not exclusively, from working-class Chinese-American families who are moderately insulated from surrounding society. In Fung's experience, such families tend to be reticent about sharing their personal lives outside the family. Research in the child language field (Heath 1986) supports Fung's experience, indicating that Chinese-Americans encourage storytelling within, but not beyond, the family circle. Thus, when she gives support to classroom teachers who wish to incorporate family stories into their first grade curriculum, Fung faces a dual challenge. As part of the school's support staff, she must persuade the first graders' families that sharing their stories with the children's classmates is not only safe but also sound educational practice. In addition, with only a limited amount of time in any given classroom, she must win the cooperation of her colleagues in order to develop an effective family stories project.

Using herself as a model and inviting colleagues and parents to observe her, Fung eventually involves a wide range of adults—teachers, parents, and school staff—in family storytelling with first graders. She audiotapes each storyteller so that children are able to listen to the stories over and over until they have learned them by heart and can retell them in their own words. Fung's results should convince even the most skeptical teachers that even in unpromising circumstances family storytelling can succeed in furthering important educational goals.

In *The Woman Warrior*, her memoir about growing up as a Chinese-American, Maxine Hong Kingston writes, "Whenever she wanted to warn us about life, my mother told stories." Calling them "stories to grow up on," Kingston evokes shadowy figures from these childhood tales and considers their influence on her own experience and that of her peers: "Those of us in the first American generations have had to figure out how the invisible world the emigrants built around our childhoods fits in solid America." Through family storytelling with Chinese-American pupils at P.S. 124, Fung begins to fit together these invisible and solid worlds, linking children, teachers, and parents together inside a new childhood tale.

It's mid-January, about a month before the start of Chinese New Year. Ms. Fung sends a note to parents of first graders, suggesting that the fifteen-day

New Year holiday, during which families traditionally gather, would be a good time to share memories and stories with their children. She believes very few of her pupils' families still tell their children the kinds of stories she heard at home as a child. She does not expect many children to bring stories from home. "But all of them will benefit from hearing the stories we tell in class." She knows that research in education indicates repeatedly that listening comprehension is the cognitive base for reading comprehension, that students who speak well are more likely to write well, and that students who have a large listening vocabulary generally sight-read with much better comprehension.

To include all the families in a way that respects cultural boundaries, Ms. Fung offers them a choice, inviting parents to share either a story or a special dish at a culminating celebration that takes place in the classroom on the last day of the New Year festivities. In the preceding weeks, Fung invites parents and interested colleagues to join her as she tells some of her own family stories to the children. Her first few storytelling sessions are brief and casual in tone. They focus on amusing topics that help her establish rapport with the children before she introduces them to more powerful themes.

"My mother always told us stories when we were growing up," Fung tells the children at the first session. "She told me one about a girl who got very smart because she ate lots of scallions. She wanted me to eat scallions too. Can you guess why?" "Why?" asks Xiu Mei, waving her hand at her teacher. "Why did she tell you to eat scallions?" Putting the Chinese words for "scallions" and "bright" on the blackboard, Fung pronounces them carefully, making sure the children hear that they sound alike. Beneath these words, she adds the words for "fish" and "plenty"—also homonyms in Chinese—which the children immediately recognize because both are present in most Chinese-American households at the Chinese New Year. Fung reminds the children that the fish on the table symbolizes plentiful food and abundance for the whole year. In the same way, she says, scallions symbolize intelligence. "When I was a child, my family wanted me to eat lots of scallions so I would be smart and have a bright future."

"Did your mother tell more stories?" one boy inquires. "Yes, lots. Next time I'll tell you the story of how I got my names." Chinese names and naming customs offer a rich source of family lore. At her next session with the children, Fung writes her birth name, her pet name, and her school name on the chalkboard in large Chinese characters, putting her family name "Fung" first, according to custom. Next to her birth name, she writes her sister's name. "When I was born my grandfather named me Kit Won Fung," she says, pointing to the characters on the board. "Kit means 'pure.' Won means 'cloud,' the same as my older sister's middle name. She is Soo Won Fung. Soo means 'simplicity.' " She points to the Chinese characters for Won. "We both have Won to show that we are in the same generation. But my father also called me 'Kam Lan.' That's his pet name for me when I was a little girl. It means 'sisterhood.' My father wanted to be sure I would get along well with my sister and with other girls." Again, she points to the relevant words on the board.

"When I started to go to school in Hong Kong, my father gave me a school name. It was 'Soo Mei,' and it means 'simply irresistible.' My mother didn't like that. She thought it was too proud. But I used the name Soo Mei until I finished fourth grade. Then we left Hong Kong and came to New York City and I didn't use it any more." After hearing Fung's name stories, the children begin doing research at home, asking their families who named them and what their names mean. They share their findings in class (see Fig. 4-1).

Chinese families, like families in other cultures, tell children stories to instill values. Chinese narrative practices, moreover, tend to make explicit references to moral and social codes, evoking confessions from children and promises not to transgress in the future (Miller, Fung and Mintz 1991). "Storytelling in my family was a kind of behavior modification technique," Fung informs her colleagues. "A story like 'Den Dai Ching Wu'—'The Frog Who's Looking Up from the Bottom of a Well'—warns about pride and boasting. It says that you live in such a confined world, you don't know what else is out there. You think you're so great, but you're only looking up from the bottom of a well. There are others greater than you, prettier, smarter. But strive for the best you can be."

As Fung talks to the children, her voice takes on a deeper, more compelling tone than before. "To teach us to show respect for our parents," she begins, "my mother told a story about a boy who loved his mother so much he would warm up the bed for her at night by sleeping in it before she did." And then she relates one of the most powerful legends in the Chinese repertoire, one that some of her colleagues might consider too disturbing to tell first graders, but that drives home the profound implications in traditional Chinese culture of the commandment to honor one's parents.

"Once there was a long and terrible famine in China. Everyone was starving. A young married woman wanted to make sure her mother-in-law would not go hungry during the famine. So she took a sharp knife and cut a piece of flesh from the soft part of her arm and put it into the soup she was cooking to feed her mother-in-law." The children listen in silence. Widely recounted in Chinese-American families (Kingston 1989; Tan 1989), this story may already be familiar to some of the children in the classroom. Fung's inclusion of it implicitly suggests it is safe for the

My name is Kar to Ip
葉嘉圖 It means good and
big plan. My dad gave me
this name because he had
a plan for me.

My name is Angela. Also, my grandfather
gave me a chinese name. My chinese
name is 劉詠琪. It mean beautiful,
always like that.

FIG. 4-1: Children's Name Pieces

youngsters to bring in traditional family stories of significance in their cultural tradition.

Once Fung has set an example by telling her own family stories, she invites her colleagues to tell theirs. The children listen attentively to all the tellers, whether or not they are gifted, whether their stories are exotic or familiar. Ms. Carmel, their classroom teacher, spins tales that stem from her childhood in Ireland and her more recent experience as an Irish immigrant. The children hear first about how she commutes each weekday from Queens to Manhattan, bringing her little son and daughter with her. While she's at work, her children stay nearby with Popo, a Chinese grandmother whose own grandchild was once in Ms. Carmel's first grade class. In Popo's house-hold, Ms. Carmel's children not only learn to enjoy Chinese cooking, but are also becoming quite fluent in the Chinese language.

"I wouldn't know what to do without Popo," Ms. Carmel tells her class. "I'm a poor Irish girl, far from home, and I didn't know how I was going to raise my children and keep on working as well. Their dad is a carpenter, much too busy to look after them while I'm teaching school. Popo treats them just the way my own grandmother would." With the children's help, Ms. Carmel begins compiling a list of family words, in Chinese and English, to post in the classroom.

"Stories are for your ears," Ms. Carmel tells the class. "The pictures are in your mind." Gathering the children on a rug at one end of the classroom, she introduces them to the magical world of Irish storytelling. Sometimes she uses Gaelic words and phrases, which she translates into English and writes down for the children to see. "In my country, we love to tell stories. Things that happen in your family become part of what we tell. In Ireland, a storyteller is called a "shanachie." The family shanachie will keep you laughing with funny stories. But Irish people love ghost stories the best." The children begin clapping their hands and calling for a ghost story. "We tell them at night," says Ms. Carmel, "by the firelight, when we're visiting with neighbors. Then we walk home in the dark, really scared." Transfixed, the children listen with rapt attention as their teacher continues.

"I'm going to tell you about a ghost story that should never have hap-pened. A story that's still told in my father's village in Ireland. It's about a haunted road and a ghost called a 'puka'—a big, dark, tall ghost that people say will take you away. But I know the puka was never on that road and I'm going to tell you why, right now. My father was learning to be a policeman, so he had to leave his village and go to school in the capital city of Dublin. That was far from the village where he lived. So he stayed in Dublin until he was finished with his work at the end of the week. Then he would come home, first on a train to the nearest big town, then on a bus to the little town of Chillee in County Kerry, and then he'd walk four miles to our village. Now all along the way he walked, there are fuchsia bushes, bushes that grow very high and fall over at the tops to make a little roof. That's handy, you know, for it keeps the rain off you when you're walking under them." Here Ms. Carmel shows the children a sketch of the fuchsia bushes that she has prepared in advance.

"In winter, when my father was walking home, it was almost always late and getting dark. In his uniform, with the dark pants and long dark coat and black hat, he looked just like a puka, the ghost that people say will take you away. People in my village are really scared of that ghost.

"One rainy night, there was my father, standing under the fuchsia bushes to get out of the rain, with his collar turned up and his black hat on, when he hears footsteps. He sees a neighbor from his village coming towards him. Well, this was a man with a limp, the only lame man in the village, so my father knew just who he was. And the man also ran under the bushes to get in from the rain, but he didn't see my father because it was dark. My father greeted him. 'How are you Michael?' said my father. 'Name of the Devil! A puka!,' cried Michael, and he ran screaming down the road. 'A puka's after me! A puka's after me!' Father was laughing and laughing because Michael was running so fast, he wasn't even limping any more."

The children in Ms. Carmel's class aren't laughing, or talking, or even moving. Sitting stock still, they wait for their teacher to finish her thrilling story.

"Well, Michael ran to my father's house in the village and he was sitting at the fireplace trying to drink a cup of tea, his hand shaking and his face as white as a sheet. When my father got home, Michael asked him, 'What road did you take? Did you see the puka?' 'No,' answered my father, 'I saw nobody.' You see, my father was afraid to tell Michael he was the one who had given him such a bad fright. 'Don't go the long road,' said Michael, 'you might meet a puka.' And that's what people in my village say to this very day."

"Is it real?" one of the girls wants to know. "Who was it?" Ms. Carmel asks the class. "Was it really a puka that night?" "Your daddy," answers another girl. "A puka's a ghost," warns a solemn looking little boy, "and they could catch you."

"Now," Fung tells the children, "listen to Ms. Carmel's story again, on the cassette, and then draw some pictures to help you remember what happens in the story. Tonight, when you go home, tell it to someone in your house. I'll teach you how to use your drawing to help you remember." She shows them how to make a little booklet from a piece of paper divided into eight squares. Each page contains two words—generally a noun and a verb—that are chosen by the child, with the teacher's help, as a key to the sequence of the story's action. The children draw a picture on each page to represent the words. They take the book home, folded up in a pocket, and use it as a guide to help them remember how to tell the story to their families.

The empathy created between children and a teacher who shares family stories with them is clearly seen in Anthony's immediate response to Ms. Carmel's family ghost story. Anthony's mother brings one of her own family ghost stories to school the very next day, along with some photographs of Anthony's grandfather and one of the haunted castles featured in the story. Fung reads Anthony's mother's story aloud to the class, and then guides Anthony as he makes a drawing and uses it to retell the story in his own words.

MY FAMILY STORY

Anthony

My family story is about my grandfather. When he was 11 years old he went to a castle with his cousins. They went there to see if the castle had any ghosts. People thought ghosts were living in the castle. There were lights in a room but the castle has no electricity. My grandpa found out they were no ghosts. They were his fishermen friends. They were playing cards, drinking, and smoking cigars. That was the end of the story.

❖ ❖ ❖ ❖ ❖ ❖ ❖ ❖ ❖

Teresa Roldan, another member of P.S. 124's support staff, tells her story the following week. She begins by asking the children how many of them live with or know their grandparents. Almost every child raises a hand. How many have never seen a grandparent? No hands are raised. "I never saw my grandfather until I was eighteen," Roldan tells the children. '*Abuelo*,' she says, pronouncing it carefully, "that's grandfather in Spanish." He lived far away in Puerto Rico, a little island far away from where I lived. So I had to wait until I was eighteen years old to save enough money to go on an airplane to Puerto Rico and see him. I was excited when I got to Puerto Rico and came out of the plane. I saw a beautiful blue sky, palm trees, and smelled the warm, sweet air. Then I met my Titi—my aunt—and she welcomed me to the land where my mommy and daddy and grandparents and great grandparents were born.

"That night I lay down in my Titi's bed and heard, 'Crik, Crik.' What's that? A little tiny tree frog called Coqui. Before the sun came up I heard a different sound, a rooster crowing. 'Titi, what's that?' There were no roosters in New York City, but there were a lot on the farm in Puerto Rico. But still, there was no abuelo.

"Later, we took a walk, going up hills and down hills, and then I saw a man wearing a straw hat and boots all the way to his knees, carrying a walking stick and pulling a cow on a rope. 'Who's that man, Titi?' 'You'll see.' The man turned his face toward us and as soon as I saw his face, I knew who he was." "Your grandfather!" several children cry out at once.

In concluding her story, Roldan tells the youngsters about how she made tape recordings of her abuelo's voice, of his stories, and of the chickens and coqui and the accordion her abuelo played. "Do you know what an accordion is?" She holds up a photograph of her grandfather. "Here is a picture of abuelo, playing his accordion." She tells the children she also made a videotape of her grandfather playing the accordion. "Can we see the tape?" asks one of the boys. Roldan says she might bring it to school. A little girl asks, "How old is your abuelo now?" "He'll be one hundred years old in March," she tells her. A boy wants to know if he's almost ready to die. "No," says Roldan, "he takes good care of himself."

In response to Ms. Roldan's story about her grandfather, a tiny first grader named Xiu Mei brings in a copy of a famous classical poem she has recently learned at Chinese school.

Journey to My Hometown

I left my hometown when I was little
I didn't return until I was older.
I could see the gray in my hair.

Even though I could still speak the language,
The children did not know who I was.
And they all asked me,
Who are you?

"When we hear family stories," Xiu Mei whispers to Fung, "it's like this poem, isn't it?" "Yes, Xiu Mei," answers her teacher. "We tell family stories to remember who we are and where we come from."

Fung encourages Xiu Mei to recite the poem to her family and then ask her grandmother to tell what meaning the famous lines have for her. The next week, Xiu Mei tries to relate her grandmother's response to the poem but doesn't quite succeed in making it clear to her teacher or her classmates. At Ms. Fung's suggestion, Xiu Mei draws a picture of the events in her grandma's story, which helps her to capture details of the story and describe them in own words. In the process, Fung leads Xiu Mei to write grandmother's story and read it to the class (see Fig. 4-2).

In subsequent sessions Fung tells the children some of her favorite folk tales, starting with a story about a patient and persevering handloom weaver who turns a single silken thread into a beautiful brocaded fabric. When Louis retells the weaver's tale at home, his mother, who speaks very little English, offers to come to the classroom and tell another folk tale, in Chinese. With Fung translating for her, she tells a Chinese version of "The Boy Who Cried Wolf." Later, Louis claims ownership of the tale by putting it into his own words: "My mother told me a story about boy who lied. Boy love to cry wolf is here. Then no one come when the wolf is here. That is why lying is not good." When Louis and his classmates ask for more folk tales, his mother returns to the classroom to tell the story "How We Got White Lines on the Black Pavement at the Crossroads."

"Long, long ago, everyone wanted to visit the animals at the big, big zoo in Hong Kong. So many cars came that traffic was dangerous. The animals had to dodge the cars and some of them got injured just the same. Lion, who was king of the zoo, got all the animals together. 'What can we do to keep ourselves from getting hurt or killed by all the cars?' he asked. 'Drivers are supposed to slow down, but they don't always see the animals. I need some volunteers to bring some order to all this traffic.' Zebra volunteered. He said it's easy to spot him, with his black and white stripes. He would stand at the crossroads, like a roadblock. So Zebra stayed at the crossroads, day and night. But after a while he needed relief. So Monkey, who is very smart, thought of a way to have Zebra's stripes at the crossroads without Zebra having to stand there at all. You know what the Monkey did?"

"He got white chalk!" the children are calling out, and laughing. "Yes," says the storyteller. "And that's how we got white lines on the black pavement at the crossroads."

As more adults come to tell their family stories to the first graders, the class collection of tape recordings grows. The children listen again and again to stories that span generations, binding them together with the adults in

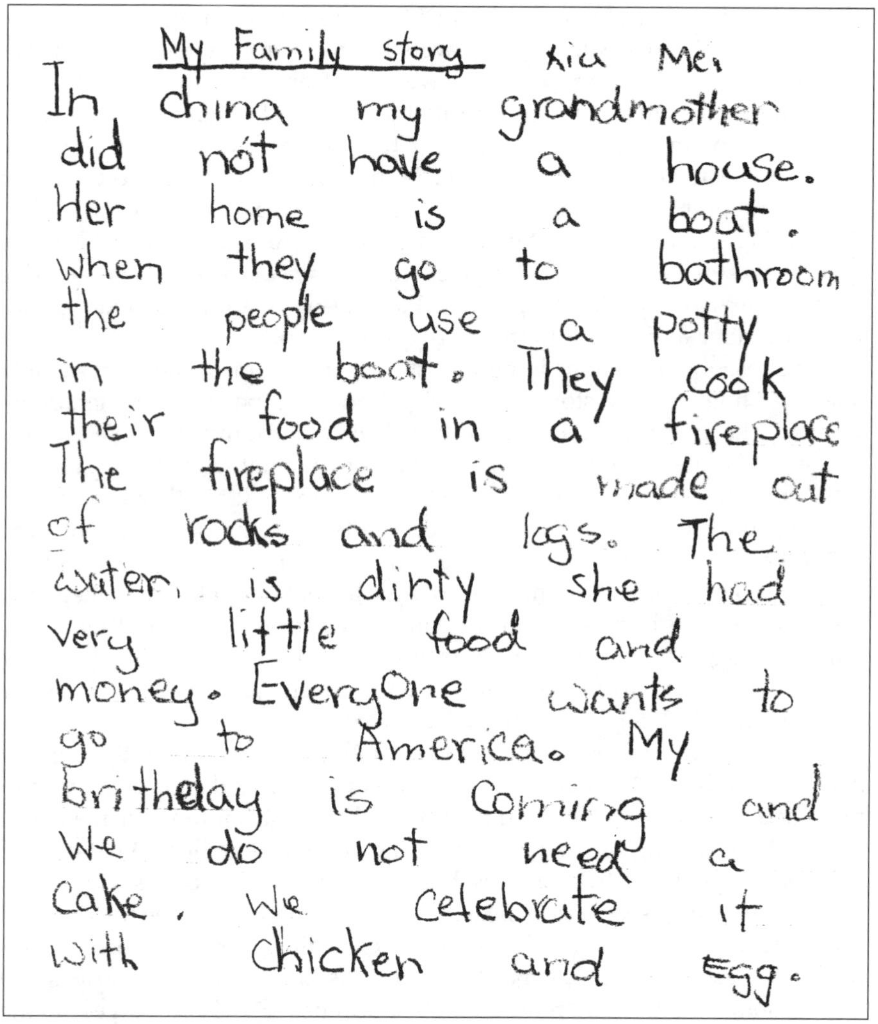

> ## My Family story   Xiu Mei
>
> In china my grandmother did nót have a house. Her home is a boat. when they go to bathroom the people use a potty in the boat. They cook their food in a fireplace The fireplace is made out of rocks and logs. The water is dirty she had very little food and money. EveryOne wants to go to America. My britheday is Coming and We do not need a cake. We celebrate it with chicken and Egg.

FIG. 4-2: My Family Story By: Xiu Mei

charge of their school lives. Patricia Carini (1986) reminds us how children beg to hear the same family stories again, "about when you were little, or the 'olden days,' or the time Daddy fell in the river, or ... the list is endless." Some of the stories they hear have power to put these young listeners in touch with experiences beyond their immediate life and times. The stories their teachers tell them strike a powerful chord in the children, not only because they are relevant to their own daily lives, but also because the stories give form to our human longing for deep roots and relatedness to others. Underscoring this theme, Carini points to "the power of collective thought, cooperative action, and, above all, human warmth and affection for developing children's strength and potential" (1986:2). Shirley Brice Heath (1983,1990), who has written extensively about the many diversities in oral and written language acquisition, points out that we still lack detailed examinations of the acquisition of structures and uses of oral languages and patterns of language socialization. Teachers who bring storytelling into the classroom have a wonderful vantage point from which to observe cultural differences in story structure, sequencing, rhythm, metaphor, and the like among their students and to reflect on their connection to the development of literacy.

On the last morning of Chinese New Year, families crowd into the school auditorium to watch the closing celebration known as the Lantern Festival. *Gung Hay Fat Choy*, the traditional New Year's greeting, adorns a banner spanning the entire width of the stage. Below it hangs a lively mural on which children have painted symbols of the New Year: Two vivid dragons loll on the left; a zodiac wheel depicting the twelve animals of the Chinese zodiac fills the center; and on the right Mickey and Minnie Mouse, dressed in traditional Chinese costumes, are standing side by side, their famished eyes fixed on an appetizing slice of Swiss cheese.

Opening ceremonies feature a parade in which artfully costumed and masked children representing the animals of the Chinese zodiac blend seamlessly with Mickey and Minnie Mouse, Donald and Daisy Duck, Bugs Bunny, and Porky Pig. These cartoon figures have become international symbols. Mythic creatures of a new generation in all four corners of the globe, they are part of the evolving story that many Chinese-American children and their families are telling about themselves at P.S. 124. Behind the animal figures, a boy and a girl dressed as Pocahontas and Captain John Smith—symbols of contact between indigenous Americans and the earliest "immigrants"—march side by side with legendary kung fu warriors and emperors and empresses.

At the conclusion of the New Year ceremonies, first grade mothers gather in Ms. Carmel's classroom, having brought holiday foods that come mainly from the famous restaurants of Chinatown and the nearby neighborhood of Little Italy. A young visitor from another classroom receives permission to join the feast because one of the children in Ms. Carmel's class is his cousin. Wearing the black cardboard rodent ears that were part of their costumes in the New Year's parade, the two cousins share fish, rice, scallions, roast pork, pizza, and homemade lasagna (from Anthony's mother) in celebration of the Year of the Rat (and Mickey Mouse). There are cakes and cookies from Chinese and Italian bakeries, and Xiu Mei's mom has made little New Year's cakes called "Fat Go." The recipe, she explains, has been handed down from her grandmother, to her mother, and then to her—a tasty addition to the family stories shared in the classroom.

READING AND WRITING MEMOIR AT P.S. 199

In Charlotte Norris's first grade classroom at P.S. 199, youngsters come from predominantly white, middle- to upper-middle-class families. Most of the children have spent their kindergarten year with Norris, so a foundation of trust already exists among teacher, children, and parents. Norris's goal is to move her first graders beyond the breakfast-to-bedtime stories they had been writing in kindergarten to more fully crafted pieces by immersing them in the study of memoir. A memoir, as William Zinsser defines it, focuses on a corner of the writer's life that was unusually vivid or intense, or that was framed by unique events: "By narrowing the lens, the writer achieves a focus that isn't possible in autobiography; memoir is a window into a life" (1987:21). Norris does not intentionally set out to develop a family stories curriculum. Like all good practitioners of memoir, however, Norris's first graders place themselves in context. As a result, their writing yields a harvest of family stories that focus on issues of importance to many six- and seven-year-olds.

Various kinds of family stories unfold simultaneously at several levels in Norris's classroom. First, since almost all these first graders have spent the previous year in her kindergarten class, there is an unusually close, quasi-familial relationship among the children and between them and their teacher. Building on this rapport, Norris quickly enlists parents' participation in classroom activities. Every Friday morning beginning at 8:45, parents spend half an hour at school reading with the children. Scattered about the room, mothers and fathers perch unsteadily on child-sized chairs or sprawl on the "meeting rug" to share picture books with their own and others' children. Several have younger children in tow. "It's part of the deal," one mother explains.

Listening intently, sometimes taking turns predicting what might happen next, and retelling familiar stories, children nestle in grown-ups' laps or press up close against their sides. "Why don't you guys read *me* a book?" one mom suggests. "And there was a bad giant and he was sleeping and in his sleep. . ." relates an excited little girl, her voice rising as she prompts her father to continue with the next page of "Jack and the Beanstalk." Sitting back-to-back with her, a solemn-looking boy holds up a comic book about a contest between superheroes and informs his father and two classmates, "Whichever side loses the most matches vanishes forever." Not far from them three classmates are listening to a father read aloud from a picture book of postcards: "P.S. I hope to see a Rocky Mountain Bighorn Sheep." "Good reading!" says one of the children.

Asked whether parents have signed up to read on a rotating basis, Norris answers that, no, they are all invited every week. "I wouldn't mind the least bit if the parents of all twenty-six kids came at the same time. If they were spilling out into the hallway, that would be fine. It's powerful for parents to read with their children in school. That shouldn't be contained within a classroom."

"I don't know of any other schools that have parents coming into first grade and interacting with their children," one mother remarks. "It's not just about fund raising. It's about helping your child in the educational process." "You get to see a lot of things going on here," adds an enthusiastic father. "I can see how to partition the work, how children get along with each other, how they must earn each other's trust. Adults probably learn through many experiences here." "It energizes you for the day," another father observes; "it's a good experience for the parents as well as the kids."

The children's parents and siblings are not the only family members who come to this first grade class to work with their youngsters. Norris's mother, a retired special education teacher, spends three mornings a week there, helping struggling readers prepare themselves for second grade; and Norris's sister, who is enrolled at the Bank Street College of Education, plans to spend part of her internship in the classroom. The class's extended family also includes Norris's colleagues from the Teachers College Writing Project where she participates in a Leadership Seminar, and Pam Allyn, a teacher-trainer at the Writing Project, has made Norris's classroom a laboratory site for the teaching of memoir.

Parents play an important role in the memoir project by helping their children record seed ideas for original memoirs in small memo notebooks. The children carry the notebooks in their pockets or knapsacks for many weeks, from school to home and back again, because the project is an experiment in family-child collaboration. Although not all parents find time to work on the notebooks, those who do clearly seem to appreciate the experience. "Every parent I speak to," Norris reports, "feels it has been of major importance to their child and to them to be able to share and learn around these personal stories." The memoir notebooks may also help children to integrate aspects of their family life in situations of divorce or in other complex family structures. For example, fathers and mothers residing in separate households can and do take turns contributing to the notebook entries. For those children whose families cannot or do not choose to participate in the project, teachers need to make alternative arrangements, perhaps by utilizing surrogate adults in the school community.

A memoir, Annie Dillard, writes, isn't "memoirs": "I wouldn't dream of writing my memoirs; I'm only forty years old." Instead, she defines a memoir as "any account, usually in the first person, of incidents that happened a while ago." Her own memoir, *An American Childhood*, is about waking up: "A child wakes up over and over again, and notices that she's living." By asking families and children to work together on memoir notebooks, Norris and Allyn, are inviting them not only to wake up and pay attention to their own lives but also, in Lucy Calkins's phrase, "to co-author a shared life and a literate world."

The teachers launch the memoir study after Thanksgiving with a sharing circle in which Allyn tells the children about her grandfather, a colorful character who wears a metal chain around his neck and once found an Indian arrowhead in his garden. As she passes the arrowhead around the circle, it sparks the memories of many children who then want to tell stories about their own relatives: Whoever holds the arrowhead is the speaker, listened to by all the others, since only one person may speak at a time. A child who has no story to tell or question to ask simply passes the arrowhead to the next person. In the weeks following, as everyone brings in objects to share—stones, shells, trinkets—and stories to go along with them, this technique proves to be valuable in managing the memoir sessions.

During the first three or four weeks of the project, Norris and the children constantly read and discuss memoir. "Not just at writer's workshop," Norris emphasizes, "but throughout the day. At read-aloud time, in morning meeting, during reading period, the memoir-reading continues. And examples of memoir in picture book format are available for parents to read with the children on Friday mornings." The readings provide a basis for group discussion about what kinds of stories are suitable for a memoir and also suggest styles and structures that might serve as models for a child's own memoir.

"We invite them to try on different styles of memoir writing," says Norris. In *When I Was Little: A Four-Year-Old's Memoir of Her Youth*, Jamie Lee Curtis depicts a child who couldn't do much as a baby but as a four-year-old could do a lot. Children identify with this theme, and the refrain that appears again and again in its pages also appeals to them. Other picture books show subjects that have inspired memoirists. *Aunt Flossie's Hats*, by Elizabeth Howard, recalls the writer's visits with her ninety-eight-year-old aunt whose hats each have a story. Cynthia Rylant's *The Relatives Came* describes a family sleepover that goes on for weeks and weeks.

Sometimes Norris reads aloud a short passage from an adult memoir, such as *The House on Mango Street* by Sandra Cisneros. Cisneros writes, "Everybody in our family has different hair. My Papa's hair is like a broom, all up in the air." On the tenth anniversary of the book's publication,

Cisneros published a Spanish-English picture book called *Hair/Pelitos*, which is based entirely on the brief passage about hair in her memoir. Norris shows the picture book to the children, comparing it with the lines she reads aloud to them from the adult version. "It looks just like she took a little bit from her notebook and made it into a memoir picture book," exclaims one child.

Norris nudges the children toward writing memoir by reminding them of the writing they did with her the year before, in kindergarten: "Last year we wrote from our own lives. We learned to write about things that were really important to us. No rainbows or hearts, remember—not from the very first day. This year we are going to pick out those times that stay with us, that you think about over and over again."

In a letter to parents that accompanies the memoir notebooks home, Norris writes that it would be best for the children to do some of the writing themselves, perhaps drawing a picture, and adding a one-sentence caption. But parents are free to take dictation from their children since the notebooks are intended primarily for recording memories. The actual writing of an original memoir will come afterward, with notebook entries serving as a basis for more fully developed individual books.

Whether or not parents help with the notebooks, the children record and share important memories in them during class time, working in pairs or small groups to facilitate discussion, with their teacher acting as moderator. Several parents who do help with the notebooks report that the assignment has given their children a chance to relive and integrate certain traumatic experiences. An entry in Brad's notebook, recorded by his mother, describes his hospitalization, which became the focus of the memoir he ultimately published (see Fig. 4-3).

Brad's mother discovers how important drawings can be in a first grader's writing. "Some of the events in Brad's memoir were expressed in pictures. For example, we took a boat and a train to get to the hospital. He put them in the pictures but not in the words." The seed idea for Zane's memoir also concerns a traumatic episode involving an important member of his family, his dog (see Fig. 4-4).

Often one child's story jogs the memories of other children. Listening to each other, children begin making their own connections. Norris initiates this conversation by telling stories about her own family, bringing in photographs of her and her siblings and her children, as well as objects she treasures. One such object is a gambling chip given to her by a cousin who worked at a casino. Soon after he gave her the chip, Norris tells the children, her cousin died in an accident. She treasures the chip because it was the last thing her cousin gave her. Since the children's imaginations are caught up by this story, Norris suggests that some of them might like to create "Me Museums," arranging their own treasured artifacts and photographs into

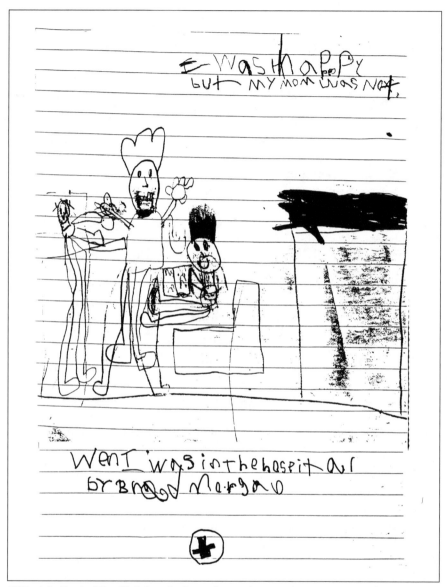

FIG. 4-3: Part of Brad's Memoir. I was happy but my mom was not when I was in the hospital. By: Brad Morgan

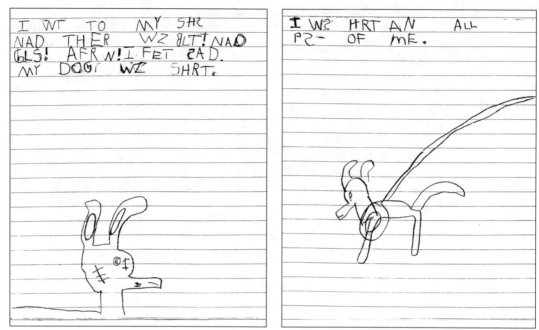

FIG. 4-4: *Part of Zane's Memoir About His Dog Jeep. [My dog Jeep jumped through a glass window.] I went to my house and there was blood! and glass! everywhere! I felt sad. My dog was hurt. I was hurt in all parts of me.*

classroom exhibits. "What does this tell us about her or him?" is the question Norris poses as a means of engaging other children, encouraging them to make inferences as they look at their classmates' displays.

Reading and discussing published memoirs, making Me Museums, and keeping and sharing memoir notebooks, the children continue working for several weeks. Their teacher hopes the process of turning their notebook entries into crafted memoir will teach the children to move beyond the breakfast-to-bedtime stories they had been writing in kindergarten. "You don't see that it's working while it's happening," she acknowledges. "You're always questioning, wondering what more you can do to move the process along."

Nudging the children from notebook entries to crafted memoir, Allyn shows them how to identify pieces they might want to expand by using Post-it notes to flag entries that seem to have connections or commonalities that can be woven together into a full memoir. Peter, for example, discovers that several entries in his notebook are about his friends. The memoir he eventually writes elaborates on the theme of spending time with friends. Sara's entries about her brother and herself, which appear side by side on facing pages in her notebook, provide the seed idea for a memoir about herself and her siblings.

Even children who struggle with reading and writing manage to work well with the notebooks. Johnny makes drawings in his notebook, adding a form of scribble writing that only he can read. His teacher elicits Johnny's stories by encouraging him to talk about the drawings, which turn out to be mostly about his mother. Johnny's final product, a memoir about himself and his mom, is told through picture stories. Jeremy, for whom English is a second language, uses a different approach. His mother, a native Spanish speaker, does her best to help him with the memoir notebook. "We talked about when he was a baby. He saw some pictures of when he was crying and he wanted to know, 'Why am I crying?' We put two pictures in his book—of Jeremy crying and Jeremy swimming." Although there is comparatively little writing in his notebook, Jeremy put in captions for the photographs. He could also have written his entries in Spanish and made the finished product into a bilingual Spanish-English memoir. Many bilingual books for children are available as models for children like Jeremy. (See Resources for Teachers.)

When the time comes for publishing and celebrating the memoir project, all the children have something to include. Many, says Norris, have been stretched as writers, overcoming painful difficulties in sounding out or writing words because the stories they wanted to tell were so important to them that they mobilized the energy and discipline to keep working.

There are several occasions by which the school and its surrounding community honor and bring closure to this schoolwide memoir project. A celebration is held at a large neighborhood bookstore where many children read their memoir books to an audience of relatives and friends. The books are put on display for a week in the school cafeteria. Throughout the week, children, parents, teachers, and school staff come to see the display. A child from each class is chosen to read a memoir aloud during a special assembly. Although choosing only one child to represent an entire class seems unfair, the assembly is a success. Norris reports: "The wonderful thing is that the entire audience, including the parents of my first graders, was made up of memoirists!"

CONTRASTS AND COMMON STRATEGIES

The contrasts and comparisons in the two classrooms described in this chapter have important implications for teachers who are interested in building educational partnerships with the families of their students. Let's begin with the contrasts. Although both storytelling and memoir call for the development of narrative skills, one places more emphasis on listening and speaking, the other on writing and reading. At the listening and speaking level, there are important differences between storytelling and memoir: storytelling typically exposes an audience to an array of genres—ghost stories, folktales, personal narratives, and tall tales—while the art of memoir involves only a single genre.

In Kit Fung's classroom, children listened again and again to adults telling different kinds of family stories, in person and on audiotapes. The children in Charlotte Norris's classroom also listened to stories, but the stories they heard were sharply focused on portions of individual lives, and they were presented as examples of ideas for a memoir, emphasizing experiences that were unusually vivid or intense or that were framed by unique events.

In both classrooms children had access to picture books, chosen to reflect the theme—whether family stories or memoir—that the group was studying. Teachers, however, presented the books with different aims in mind: One used picture books mainly for their *content*, with the aim of creating and sustaining the youngsters' enthusiasm for gathering family stories; the other provided the children with books chosen to help them gain a deeper understanding of the *style* and *structure* of memoir.

Families collaborated with children and teachers in both settings, but with different levels of comfort (probably on the part of teachers as well as parents) about actually participating in the classroom. For cultural as well as practical reasons, only a few parents of the Chinese-American first graders took part in the family stories project. Those who did waited until adults in the school had provided a structure and an impetus by sharing their own stories and teaching the children to retell them at home. Parents of the white, middle-class children, on the other hand, who were already accustomed to participating in weekly read-aloud sessions in the classroom, became actively involved in helping their children record ideas for memoir in their notebooks.

In each case, teachers used common strategies to advance curricular aims. Whole-class and small-group discussions among teachers and children were important throughout both projects. The use of children's drawings was central for eliciting details that enriched and expanded their narratives; it also helped them remember and retell important events in proper sequence. Planning and teamwork with colleagues and parents was also crucial to the success of both projects. Parents, like teachers, through their observations of and conversations with the children, gained understanding about the process of learning and teaching. And celebrations that honored the children's work were important in bringing closure to both projects.

Strategies that help make one of the projects successful can also be effective in the other. Teachers and parents in the memoir project, for example can make tape recordings of their favorite passages from adult memoir, thus utilizing the techniques of storytelling. Families and children in the storytelling project can use notebooks to record memorable family stories and, equally important, the children's responses to them. Finally, teachers can extend the intergenerational aspect of both projects by having children work with various adults in the school to supplement, or when necessary to substitute for, the work they do with their parents.

5

Home Cooking

Good old hot rolls with homemade butter and homemade preserves. As soon as I'd finish one, I'd say, "Mama, thank you for another roll," and she'd put one on my plate.

—*Eloise Greenfield and Lessie Jones Little*

At most elementary schools, family involvement in classroom cooking begins and ends with a Parents Association Bake Sale. Jennifer Tuten uses approaches to cooking in school that offer refreshing departures from this pattern.

Tuten's cooking curriculum for third and fourth graders at the Corlears School in Manhattan's Chelsea district began when she spent six weeks at the National Endowment for the Humanities Summer Folklore Institute at Bank Street College. At the institute, she developed a methodology for exploring bread and soup as a literature-based curricular theme that includes not only cooking with parents and children in the classroom, but also oral history, folktales, and proverbs related to bread and soup—foods that are basic in a wide range of cultures.

Tuten emphasizes the ways in which cooking integrates various aspects of the curriculum: Reading, writing, mathematics, chemistry, history, geography, and problem solving are all potential ingredients of any recipe. Her students learn to read recipes from various types of cookbooks and write their own class cookbook. They also read and write about cooking and food in a range of literary genres. In mathematics, they learn to double the amounts of ingredients in recipes, divide them in half, predict what will happen when they use unspecified amounts—adding slowly to see how much flour, for example, is needed to make other ingredients stick together. Comparing the process of making breads from recipes that do or do not call for yeast teaches them something about chemistry. Learning to follow directions and experiment with the effects of adding or subtracting ingredients are exercises in problem solving. Mapping the countries where family recipes originated and comparing related recipes from different countries are the basis for a geography lesson.

In a school like Corlears, which attracts students from a range of ethnic and economic backgrounds, traditional recipes handed down from one generation to another are a natural link to family histories and countries of origin. They personalize and individualize the concept of immigration. As Tuten's students and their families collaborate on a cookbook that features breads and soups, plus some desserts, they learn to appreciate both the similarities and the differences among the recipes and the traditions they represent.

Before beginning to collect recipes from relatives, her class examines cookbooks written for children, with special attention to books that introduce readers to the geography and food traditions of various island cultures. (See Resources for Teachers for a list of books relevant to a cooking curriculum.) The children also consult published guides to collecting family histories as sources of tips for carrying out interviews with family cooks. For example, Zimmerman (1988: 47) suggests asking, How does our family prepare for and celebrate special holidays, such as Christmas, Easter, Three Kings Day, Ramadan, Passover, Chanukah? What special foods do we eat? What traditions do we follow? What is your recipe to prepare that wonderful (name dish) you make for Thanksgiving or Christmas? How do you prepare (other dishes)? Davis (1993:14) proposes a different question: Can you remember a time when you tried to cook something and it didn't turn out?

Greene and Fulford's chapter on food (1993:118–124) lists forty-two questions for family members, among them: What recipe are you famous for? What do you prepare for a small group? for a large group? What dish do you usually bring to a potluck or a picnic? What microwave food do you find tasty? What cookbook do you use most? Which one do you remember your mother using? What do you remember about your first trips to a grocery store? To a supermarket? What was the most delicious meal you've ever had? Are you allergic to any foods? Is there anything you cannot stand or will not eat? Questions like these are incorporated into a survey questionnaire for students to use in collecting information and recipes from family members.

The children practice interviewing each other in pairs and also interview volunteers from the school staff, honing their skills and further developing their lists of questions. The theme—bread and soup—structures the children's recipe collecting in ways that allow them to make comparisons across different traditions, which is one of the project's goals. However, Tuten underscores the importance of accepting and exploring all the recipes that come in (whether or not they fit the theme), thus avoiding the pitfall of taking only recipes that reflect cultural stereotypes. "Inclusion is the goal," she says. "When a Korean child brings in a recipe for non-Korean food, I don't try to persuade her to bring a Korean one instead. Her choice—or her family's choice—may very well be an important expression of cultural identity or accommodation to a new culture, whether or not it fits my expectations." Recipes that use prepared mixes for breads or cakes are also acceptable, because family cooks often rely on these shortcuts to save time in the midst of busy lives.

Throughout the project, Tuten and the children broaden their understanding of how human beings "turn the consumption of food, a biological necessity, into a carefully cultured phenomenon" (Visser 1991: ix) by studying folktales about food, such as McGovern's *Stone Soup*, tales about magic pots, and folklore about cooks, recipes, food riddles, and even spells. They also read trickster tales like the "Gingerbread Boy" or Johnnycake stories. Examining similarities and differences among the versions of a particular tale, as it is told in different countries, augments the comparative study of how bread and soup are prepared in various places.

In addition, the children study proverbs about food and cooking and develop improvisations to express both their literal and metaphoric meanings. On Grandparents Day, proverbs posted on the walls decorate the classroom: A watched pot never boils. Too many cooks spoil the broth. Many hands make light work. Don't cry over spilt milk. Don't count your chickens before they hatch. Don't put all your eggs in one basket. Some children perform skits based on their favorite proverbs. Many also elicit recipes, and the memories associated with them, from their grandparents.

Tuten's classroom contains a corner with a sink, counter top, shelves, and a convection oven. When necessary, the class has access to a larger oven in the school's basement kitchen. A student teacher from a local college is usually available to assist with classroom cooking. To no one's surprise, the most successful cooking sessions are those in which parents are involved. Using a hot plate, a toaster oven, and, sometimes, a convection oven, the children prepare approximately half the recipes that the group has collected, and they enjoy eating the results. Students who sign up for a particular session cook in groups of four or five; other classmates come by and have a look when they are not otherwise occupied. Everyone has at least one chance to cook.

"Parents enjoy the cooking as much as the children do," asserts Tuten. A parent like Rosina's mother, Carmen, who speaks very little English and has always seemed timid and uncomfortable at Corlears, discovers that cooking in the classroom makes her feel a part of, rather than apart from, the school. Rosina's pride in her mother's accomplishments also has a positive effect on Rosina's self-esteem. Carmen begins by insisting that the children clean the sink, counter top, and shelves. "We thought it was pretty clean," says one fourth grader, "but she made us rearrange everything. She acted like a real chef." Tuten agrees: "She gave orders to her group, and they loved it. She demonstrated techniques—peeling and slicing vegetables for soup—

A FAMILY FOOD TRADITION

recipes from Jenny Tuten's 8/9s

LEBKUCHEN

CONTRIBUTED BY: ALBERT

RECIPE SOURCE: His parents, Robert & Nancy

INGREDIENTS

1 cup molasses
1 cup brown sugar
1 tbsp baking soda

2 tbsp brandy
2 eggs
1 tbsp aniseed
1 tsp each: cinnamon, ginger, nutmeg, cloves, allspice
1/2 tsp each: cardomon and salt
1/4 tsp white pepper
1/4 lb each: citron and orange peel, cut fine
1/4 lb almonds, cut in large pieces

4 - 4 1/2 cups all-purpose flour

DIRECTIONS

Boil first 3 ingredients for a minute in a large saucepan. Cool. Add rest of ingredients, except flour. Combine. With heavy wooden spoon, add enough flour to make a stiff dough. Pat into a 12" x 18" x 1" pan, very well greased. A little flour dusted over dough makes it easier to even out. Bake at 350 for 20 minutes. Turn out onto a board and when cool cut into pieces. A soft icing flavored with lemon juice or brandy may be spread on it while warm, before cutting.

NOTES

Clare Konig brought this recipe from Germany to America in the '20s and gave it to Bob's family. Nancy sometimes adds crystallized ginger, but Bob still thinks Clare made it the best. He's glad she stayed in Connecticut and missed the fighting of World War II.

A FAMILY FOOD TRADITION

recipes from Jenny Tuten's 8/9s

DOMINICAN CHICKEN SOUP

CONTRIBUTED BY: Rosina

RECIPE SOURCE: Her mother, Carmen

INGREDIENTS

1 chicken
2 carrots
3 potatoes
1 lb cassaba
1/4 lb noodles
2 chicken boullion cubes
1 spoon vinegar
1 small onion
garlic
3 liters of water

DIRECTIONS

Cut the chicken in pieces. Put everything in a big pot and put it on the stove. Add the salt as you like it.

NOTES

This recipe originated in the Dominican Republic more than 30 years ago. It's served on special occasions. Rosina thinks her mom makes it the best.

A FAMILY FOOD TRADITION

recipes from Jenny Tuten's 8/9s

LONGEVITY SOUP

CONTRIBUTED BY: Emma

RECIPE SOURCE: Grandma

INGREDIENTS

1 head chickory
5 peeled carrots
2 large peeled potatoes
a small handful of parsley
1 parsnip

DIRECTIONS

Cut up all the vegetables and add 1 quart water. Boil in large pot 1-1 1/2 hours. Puree in blender. Add salt and butter. Eat with French bread.

NOTES

Emma's grandfather lived to be 97 years old. He attributed his good health to this French soup (also made by his many friends), which he ate 2-4 times a week.

FIG. 5-1: Recipes From A Family Food Tradition

with Rosina translating what she said. It was the first time I've ever seen Carmen in authority. She was not a bit timid. And Rosina, who usually seems burdened by having to translate for her mother, was so proud and happy to do it!"

Publication of a class cookbook marks the culmination of the cooking project. The third and fourth graders celebrate their cookbook at a school fair, selling autographed copies to help raise money for the school. *A Family Food Tradition: Recipes from Jenny Tuten's 8/9s* includes recipes for Dominican chicken soup, cupcakes for holidays and special occasions, Czech rye bread, hazelnut butter cookies, couscous cake, pumpkin pie, dumpling soup, Irish beef stew, potatoes with chorizo, matzohball soup, lebkuchen, and a French vegetable soup called longevity soup. Almost all have been passed down in the children's families, sometimes from great-grandparents to grandparents to parents and, now, to a new generation (see Fig. 5-1).

When asked what she might do differently next year, Tuten says she would spend more time on the cooking curriculum. "There was such a rush to get the book done in time for the Christmas fair that the children got short-changed: I would have liked them to type the recipes but there wasn't time, so a couple of the parents did it instead. But the kids got to make the cover. They liked doing that, and autographing all the books."

Teachers who do not have as much time or as many resources as Tuten can adapt her approach by using a hot plate and a toaster oven, or they can encourage families to prepare foods at home and bring them into the class-room to share. At P.S. 24 in Queens, for example, Robin Kruter holds an annu-al Bread Festival for her first graders and their families at the conclusion of a year-long food curriculum. She asks parents to prepare traditional breads at home and then bring them to share with the children in school at an afternoon coffee, tea, cocoa, and soda pop party that features breads from a dozen different countries along with white bread from the local supermarket. As Margaret Visser notes in her book *The Rituals of Dinner*, "We use eating as a medium for social relationships: satisfaction of the most individual of needs becomes a means of creating community." Bringing home cooking to the classroom gives teachers a chance to share this powerful experience with their students and their students' families.

6

Coming to America

*Families often tell a migration saga as the
first real narrative in the history of a family.*

—Steven Zeitlin

It isn't often that a group of adults is genuinely moved by a grade school play. However, dramatizations of immigration stories, based on the experiences of the children or their families, are the exception. While there may be some tears throughout the house, the people who aren't crying generally have smiles as wide as the rivers or oceans they've crossed.

At P.S. 75, parents of Ted Kesler's third graders were spellbound by the presentation that concluded the children's study of immigration. Slide photographs of the third graders proudly holding handmade puppets that represented immigrants from many different countries flashed by as the children's voices, recorded on audiotape, read aloud from their original stories of the immigrants' journeys to America and their struggle to realize the American Dream. When some of the grown-ups in the audience started crying, it was clear that something special was happening in Class 3-223.

It had begun the previous summer, when Kesler attended the Folklore Institute at Bank Street College. His goal was to prepare an immigration study that would draw not only on the rich resources of New York City, but also on the experiences of his students and their families. Early in the fall, after meeting with parents to discuss the immigration study and their potential contribution to it, Kesler and the children began listing "The Countries

We Come From" and the numbers of families from each country on a large sheet of chart paper. They included the following countries:

Ireland (1)   Dominican Republic (2)

Czechoslovakia (1)   Russia/Ukraine (8)

Israel (1)   Brazil (1)

Hungary (2)   Lithuania (2)

India (3)   China (4)

Japan (1)   England/Scotland (3)

Trinidad (1)

A large map of the world, pinpointing all the countries of origin, was propped on an easel at the front of the classroom (see Fig. 6-1).

FIG. 6-1: Map

Nearby hung another chart that listed the number of children who spoke each of "The Languages Spoken in Families of Class 3-223."

English (30)	Mandarin (2)
Polish (3)	Albanian (1)
Hindi (1)	Russian (2)
Spanish (8)	Yiddish (5)
French (1)	German (3)
Japanese (1)	Hebrew (3)
Punjabi (1)	

Learning about immigration through a study of their own heritage, the students in Kesler's class personalized a social process that affects people in every part of the world. Whether involuntary, as in the case of slavery, or voluntarily for economic, political, and/or religious reasons, immigration and migration touch us all. Laura Schiller (1996:46–51), whose year-long study, "Coming to America," created a strong sense of community among her diverse middle school students, suggests several important reasons for focusing on family stories in a study of immigration. "I would invite stories about our ancestors, our heritage, slavery, and immigration from both parents and students, written in whatever language the authors felt most comfortable. I wanted to model that literacy is valuable in all languages, not just English, and everyone, regardless of ability, can participate." She also chooses to focus on immigration because of its prominence in the news: "In a TV special, Walter Cronkite dubbed immigration *the* issue of the twenty-first century. Spawning racism, scapegoating, and controversy worldwide, immigration could take many directions and involve many points of view. We could be part of the ongoing dialogue in the government and media."

At the outset, Kesler asked each of his third graders to work with a parent on a time line of the child's own life, noting an important event for each year. As a follow-up assignment, the children interviewed family members and created time lines for a parent or other relative. Reviewing the time lines in class and pointing out that significant events often involved *moving*, Kesler helped the children connect their own or their family's experiences of moving with the immigration stories they were beginning to read and hear about in class.

In a related activity, their teacher asked them to find out how they got their names and what meanings their names had. The children produced such rich and diverse responses that Kesler compiled them in a class book of name stories. The book was so popular that every child wanted an individual copy to take home (see Fig. 6-2).

Throughout the immigration study, Kesler and the children read and discussed many wonderful picture books with an immigration theme. "At the center of each book, there's someone the kids' age," Kesler points out, "so that they're much more likely to make a connection with the experience of immigration than they might otherwise." After discussing the books in groups of three or four, children worked together on writing comments about them that clearly show the role of picture books in opening their imaginations to the experience of immigration (see Fig. 6-3).

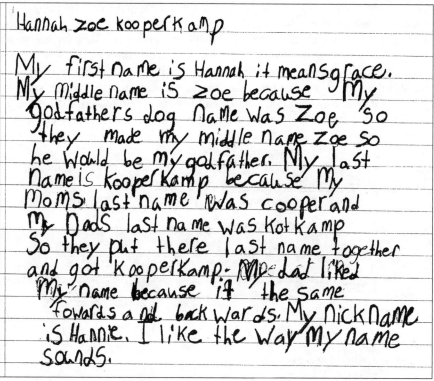

FIG. 6-2: Hannah's Name Piece. Hannah Zoe Kooperkamp
My first name is Hannah. It means grace. My middle name is Zoe because
my godfather's dog's name was Zoe. My last name is Kooperkamp because
my mom's last name was Cooper and my dad's last name was Kotkamp.
They put their last names together and got Kooperkamp. My dad likes
my name because it is the same forwards and backwards. My nickname
is Hannie. I like the way my name sounds.

Current visions of authorship and development (Applebee 1993; Dyson 1993) emphasize the importance of a thematically substantive language arts curriculum, one concerned not just with individual work but with collective conversations about ideas that matter (see also Dyson 1995). In Kesler's class the focal point of these conversations, reflected in class discussion and in what the children were reading and writing, was on the connections between families and immigration. Guided by their teacher, the children compared the immigration stories they read with the ones they heard from their parents and other adults, in class and at home.

To begin teaching the children how to do an interview about immigration with a family member, Kesler modeled the process several times in class, interviewing his own father and then six class parents over a period of several weeks. After reflecting on which questions brought the most interesting answers, the class discussed interview techniques, such as how to ask productive questions, how to make interviewees comfortable, and how to tape record an interview. Kesler also modeled the rudiments of notetaking during the interviews he conducted in class, taking notes on large sheets of newsprint that were clipped to an easel for everyone to see. At the conclusion of this phase, the children used these notes to make charts comparing information from all the interviewees.

> Class 3-22 5. Immigration study, October, 1994.
> Group Members: ① Emily Nord-Podberesky ② Alexandra Kiesman
> ③ Anthony Lopez ④
>
> Book title: The Wooden Doll
> Author: Suson Bonners Illustrator: Susan Bonners
>
> What we discovered about immigration from this book:
>
> We discovered that a lot of people take special things with them when they immigrate. A lot of people miss people that they leave behind when they immigrate. Sometimes they keep reminders. He left Poland because they had to work to hard

FIG. 6-3: Immigration Book Report

As a next step, each child worked with a partner to develop a list of questions for an immigrant interview. After Kesler approved the lists, the children were ready to interview a family member or family friend who had an immigration story to tell. Next, using the material from their interviews, the children rewrote the stories as first-person accounts (see Fig. 6-4).

One parent volunteered to teach the children how to make puppets to represent the individuals whose immigration experiences they had recorded and were presenting in their first-person narratives. Her directions for making the pâpier maché puppets are as follows:

Pâpier Maché Immigrant Puppets

I will never forget what they looked like after they were finished, each one standing on the desk of the child who had made it as a kind of silent yet vital testimony to that child's heritage.

> Marlene Streisinger, mother of Kinu Yamamato.

Preparation

1. I made thirty-two pâpier maché heads out of balloons and newspaper.
2. We held a class discussion in which children decided what part of the world each of their puppets would come from, what they would look like physically. I showed the class a Japanese puppet I made as a sample.
3. We decided on, listed, and gathered materials.

Workshop Session One: Heads, Necks, Faces

1. Each child received a pâpier maché balloon head, learned to handle it gently.
2. We drew mouths, eyes, ears, noses, mustaches on cardboard and cut them out.
3. I explained what pâpier maché was and we practiced soaking newspaper strips in the mixture so that it became moldable and we got used to the feeling of cold, gloppy flour and water solution.
4. We covered each feature with pâpier maché and affixed them to the heads to make faces.
5. We secured the heads onto necks made of cardboard tubes covered with more pâpier maché strips. The key: make each head/neck unit a balanced piece of sculpture in itself that will stand alone without tipping over.
6. Set on window sill to dry.

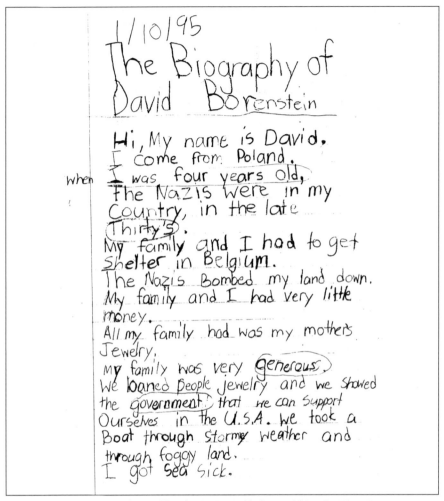

FIG. 6-4: *Morris's Profile of His Grandfather Told in the First Person*
The Biography of David Borenstein

Hi, my name is David. I come from Poland. When I was four years old, the Nazis were in my country. This was in the late thirties. My family and I had to get shelter in Belgium. The Nazis bombed my land down.

My family and I had very little money. All my family had was my mother's jewelry. My family was very generous. We loaned people jewelry and showed the government that we could support ourselves in the U.S.A.

We took a boat through stormy weather and through foggy land. I got sea sick.

Workshop Session Two: Bodies, Costumes

1. Classroom teacher and parent cut arm and neck holes into the sides and tops of empty seltzer bottles, using Xacto knives.
2. The children put heads and armholes into the appropriate holes and glued them on.
3. Children painted faces with flesh-tones-of-the-world tints.
4. Children measured, cut, glued on colored yarn for hair.
5. Class selected puppets' costumes from 32 basic T-shaped garments that Ms. Streisinger had sewn. Children chose fabrics from scrap stash, measured, cut, sewed, and glued kerchiefs and other head-dresses, aprons, vests, capes, belts, sarongs, and the like to suit each puppet's body size and ethnicity.

Workshop Session Three: Mitten Hands, Accessories

1. Teacher and parent traced four mittens shapes onto flesh tone felt with tailor's chalk and cut them out.
2. Experimenting, they sewed two pairs of mitten hands using different types of stitches.
3. They stuffed each pair of mitten hands with cotton to shape them, and then glued them to the ends of puppets' arms.
4. They discussed ways of cutting out and sewing cloth flowers, decorating puppets with feathers, beads.
5. They led the class through these steps.

The finished puppets, treasured by the children, were proudly loaned to the school library, where they were put on display for several weeks. Later, they were featured in an audiovisual presentation that was part of the ceremony marking the close of the study. At that ceremony, the children's work was displayed around the classroom. It included time lines; family trees; maps of countries of origin and languages spoken by members of the children's families; name stories; posters reviewing picture books on immigration themes; interviews; snapshots of the class neighborhood walks, during which students interviewed several local merchants who were recent immigrants to the United States; and accounts of the class trip to Ellis Island. The children's summaries of the immigration study reflected on the work they had done, and suggested which parts of the study had been most important to them.

An Immigration Work Report Card gave the third graders an opportunity for self-assessment and, simultaneously, provided a chronological outline of the various tasks involved in the project, so that the children and their families could see how much they had done and could take pride in what they had accomplished (see Fig. 6-5).

Immigration Work Report Card. Class 3-223. Name: L/c) Baysock		
Work We Did	Grade (from 1 to 10)	Reason
Time Lines	10	I wrote alot of things that happened.
How I Got My Name	9	I wrote neatly the seconed time.
Family Tree	10	I added on the three more relatives that I needed to.
Picturebook Work	10	I tried to work with my group. And we didn't have alot of problems.
Immigrant Interview Chart	10	I wrote alot of reasons why they came, for each person.
Immigrant Interview Worksheet	10	Everything I wrote down is true.
Field Trip Work	9	I didn't finish everything.
Newspaper Articles	10	I brought in alot of articles.
Immigrant Puppet	10	I put alot of work into it.
Immigrant Story	10	I put alot of work into it.

Overall Grade ⟶ 10

Write 3 reasons.
Use the back if necessary!

(1.) I only got two grade nines.
(2.) I put alot of work into all of the assignments.
(3.) I'm very proud of all my work!!!
(4.) I did my best. (5.) I wrote neatly.

FIG. 6-5: Immigration Work Report Card

Making the children's families central to the immigration study took courage. Some children and/or their families were hesitant to share information they felt was painful or private. Although he scrupulously respected everyone's needs and made sure they were comfortable, Kesler reports that "almost everyone stretched to accommodate the goals of the project." For children to trust their teacher in a study of immigration that personalizes the content, the teacher must be willing to take some risks and become self-revealing too. Kesler accompanied his students every step of the way. He contributed to the class book on names, he persuaded his own father to be interviewed in the classroom, and he opened himself to the children and their families, delighting in the different worlds they represented, and showing enthusiastic interest in them and in their ideas. In the process, he enlarged the meaning of community in his classroom and, perhaps equally important, he helped his students begin to understand how human beings, often with courage and a sense of adventure, continually construct and reconstruct their worlds.

7

Elders Share Their Lives

*Miss not the discourse
of the elders.*

—*Ecclesiastes*

In traditional societies the elders of a community, respected and consulted for their wisdom and experience, help guide the young. In America today, migration, mobility, broken families, and the lure of mass communication often erode opportunities for young and old people to spend time together in meaningful ways. "Because our family structures are being torn apart," says Susan Perlstein, director of Elders Share the Arts (ESTA), "youths and the elderly don't even see one another. An elementary school and senior citizen center partnership teaches all involved to value relationships in our community. A broader definition of family includes community" (Perlstein 1995).

Teachers who make a commitment to bring seniors into the classroom or to bring classes together with senior centers take on a big challenge. Steven Zeitlin calls it "one of our greatest challenges: to take traditional intergenerational activities which once provided such nourishment and sustenance, and to find ways to reestablish them, more self-consciously, but with no less passion or validity in the modern institutions of school and senior center" (Zeitlin 1993:11).

The challenge is great but the rewards can be even greater as teachers and children discover that schools and senior centers are no less valid settings for nurturing ties between the generations than a grandmother's kitchen or the front porch. ESTA offers intergenerational workshops, training, performances, and festivals across the country to teachers and community-service professionals working with many different populations. In addition, lively and detailed accounts of kids and seniors working together are available. *Generating Community* (Perlstein and Bliss 1994) describes many ESTA projects; *Nourishing The Heart* (Davis and Ferdman 1993) outlines a range of successful collaborative projects with suggestions for how teachers might adapt them to the needs of their own classes. (See Resources for Teachers.)

This chapter focuses on ESTA-sponsored partnerships between elementary school children and members of senior citizens' centers in two New York City boroughs: Bedford-Stuyvesant, Brooklyn; and Flushing, Queens. In Bedford-Stuyvesant, African-American and Caribbean-American seniors from a range of cultures and nationalities are paired with third graders at a public school that many of the elders had themselves attended as kids. The Flushing project pairs Asian, Middle Eastern, Bosnian, African-American, and Latino fifth graders from Public School 24 with predominantly Eastern European Jewish elders.

Using a synthesis of oral history and theater arts, ESTA works with teams of teachers and artists as well as families, friends, and volunteers to help children and seniors design and carry out living history presentations that address local community issues. "You won't see dazzling sets, lights, costumes, and dramaturgy in an ESTA performance," says Joanne Schultz, coordinator of ESTA's intergenerational program. "What you'll see is a person or a group enacting a very meaningful personal story. You'll see previously untold stories, hidden history, being revealed, whether about the hassles of deaf people at the Department of Motor Vehicles or about kids who mug senior citizens. And you'll always see audiences from the community enjoying themselves and responding with recognition to what they see" (Schultz 1994: 43).

Often ESTA artists have experience in alternative theater. This includes traditional storytelling, social theater (staged in settings like labor unions), performance art (emphasizing autobiography and new performance forms), and postmodern dance (which uses everyday movements and "non-dancers"). These diverse backgrounds allow them to offer ways of creating theater that are inexpensive, expressive, and accessible.

Working primarily with oral language, ESTA's approach parallels studies of literacy acquisition that suggest that negotiated, socially interactive, and oral aspects of language support children in the passage to literacy (Schieffelin and Gilmore, 1986). As the third graders and fifth graders described here develop mutual trust with the seniors, they also gain self-confidence and self-esteem. In addition, the fifth graders—even those for whom English is a relatively new language—also take pleasure in writing about "my senior."

Beginning in the fall, an ESTA artist or theater person spends five weeks working with children in their classroom and, separately, with older adults at the senior center. During this period, the children learn interviewing techniques by doing interviews with their parents or other adult relatives. They work out family trees and stories from these interviews. "Many of the children are not native-English speakers and they were hesitant about writing in English when school began," says fifth grade teacher Susan Maloney. "Once they started working with Joanne, making family trees and practicing interviewing skills on their parents, they became more confident."

Initial workshops with the elderly focus on helping them overcome fears of being disrespected or dismissed by the youngsters. Sometimes there are racial and cultural biases that need to be discussed. After the first five weeks, the seniors and youngsters begin working together to transform their experiences and life histories into art. "The most difficult aspect of the intergenerational arts program," explains Schultz, "is working with people who don't have the habit of art-making in their daily lives. They don't have a way of working, and they have to learn it. Finding a creative working process is like learning to walk. It is necessary to teach them that this process is not instant; it takes time and needs development."

Engaging in a collaborative process, both children and elders recall experiences and discover abilities they might otherwise not have realized they had. Transcending age barriers and cultural stereotypes, they restore the connections between youth and age that are essential to a caring community.

EXPLORING CONNECTIONS: THIRD GRADERS AND SENIORS IN BROOKLYN

In Bedford-Stuyvesant, Brooklyn, actress Dawn Formey, known to her pupils as Ms. D., is working with a group of African-American youngsters from Yvonne Gunn's third grade class at the Bedford Village School. Below freezing temperatures, icy streets, and biting winds have kept the seniors at home today, so Ms. D. and the children are on their own. The workshop is usually held at the Bedford branch of the public library, across the street from the school. Today Ms. D. and the children are using Gunn's sunny, colorful classroom instead. They have pushed all the chairs to one end of the room, clearing a space large enough for movement exercises. Gunn joins the children as Ms. D. leads them through a series of rhythmic, coordinated movements. By using a vernacular English familiar to children from Bedford-Stuyvesant, Ms. D. immediately establishes a relationship to them as an acting coach and a performance artist from the community theater, as distinct from a classroom teacher. Her aim is to make the children feel comfortable enough to let their natural talents and enthusiasm emerge.

"You should have your knees bent, just slightly. Your feet should be right under your knees. Head moves. Fingers snapping. 1-2-3-4, up-2-3-4, and right-2-3-4, and left-2-3-4." The children follow attentively. "Now, we ready? Huh? Shake the whole body!"

Tongue twisters come next. "We gon' go through some tongue twisters," says Ms. D. "So, can I have a silent scream. And *release* that face. Now—hello—move those lips. And the big black bug beat the big black bear and the big black bear bled blood." Laughing, the children struggle to finish the sentence. "Y'all are too relaxed," Ms. D. complains. They repeat the twister, this time with growly bear faces and arms raised in threatening poses. "Now louder. Now whisper. Now stage whisper, a little bit more than just a regular whisper. Good! Some of you got it. Some of you are a little scared. Are you gonna loosen up and be a part of the whole? Good!"

Maintaining a rapid pace, Ms. D. tells the class they will work on transitions from one position to another. She allows time for each person to pick four basic positions, then counts them through all four, slowly at first. "Y'all gotta *remember* it." Soon, almost everyone can switch positions at Ms. D.'s command (1-2-3-4, 2-1-3-4, and so on). "Now we gettin' good. Now, go to your next movement as *cool* as possible. Meaning coordination. Y'all ready? I want you to *hold* it. *No* other movement. Take your time gettin' to it."

Distracted, one of the boys begins talking to a classmate. Putting her arm around his shoulders, Ms. D. takes him out of the group. "What's wrong, bugga? You understand exercise? One movement. One thing. Ain't a whole buncha nothing. *Slow*. Like the karate flicks." The boy laughs. "I'm *serious*!" She sends him back to his place, telling the group to put all their attention, all their energy into what they're doing. Treating the children as if they were professional theater people, she lets them know she has confidence in their abilities. "Take your time. You can do it. Y'all smart now."

When attention wanders, when children talk or tease one another, Ms. D. invokes a call-and-response derived from African tradition to bring them back into focus: "AH-GO," she calls.(It means "Are you here?") "AH-MAY" ("I'm listening"), the children reply. Next, as she forms the youngsters into opposing groups for a tug-of-war using an imaginary rope, she tells them,"If you cannot participate in the group I put you in, then sit down. You're not in." A child in the audience complains that the sun is in his eyes. "You got sun in your face? You be glad! What would you do if the sun didn't come out?" Then, addressing one of the tug-of-war teams she says, "This group has a problem. I don't *believe* y'all holdin' the same rope. Problem here with the imagination. Get into that rope. Now, this group is winnin', What should be happening, physically, to your bodies?" Within a few minutes, audience and players switch places. "Action! Pull! Pull that rope! Now: freeze!"

Taking the children through an ensemble-theater exercise, Ms. D. transforms the tug-of-war teams into "circles of unity." One group is now Apples, and the other is Oranges. "You're together. You love each other. Stickin' together." Forming the Apples and Oranges into two separate clusters, she explains that she wants them to move toward each other, then away from each other, sticking tightly together in their clusters. "This is a tug-of-war of *minds*. Show them your meanest look. No sound, just action in the face. It's a war zone."

Spontaneously, both groups begin boasting of their qualities. "We look good." "We taste better." "We are tasty." "We sweet, sweet all the way!" Delighted, Ms. D. says, "Good! That's the drama we need. But it's gotta go back and forth, so the audience can understand. Action—reaction." Carried away with enthusiasm, the Apples shout, "Charge!" Dawn stops them; then she reconsiders. "That's good. Say 'Charge.' Sometime Ms. D. gotta learn from y'all." But she tells them their groups are "still too linear, not a cluster." The scene continues, with Apples and Oranges moving back and forth, then merging and laughing. "Merge! Freeze! Giggle!" Ms. D. commands. Now an Apple and an Orange pop out from each group and stare at each other in silence. "Fall out. Face each other. Pretend to punch each other in the face. Then hug and one of you say 'Apple,' the other say 'Orange.'"

The workshop ends. Next week, the third graders will resume working with the seniors at the neighborhood branch of the public library.

At lunch in the teachers' room, Ms. D. asks Ms. Gunn, the classroom teacher, how the children are coming along with their family trees. Gunn reports that it isn't working. "A lot of them don't even know the last names of parents or grandparents." She feels this is one reason why some children are already calling the seniors "grandma" or "grandpa" and fighting to sit next to one of them. "Ownership," she says. "The kids have trouble sharing their seniors with each other."

In the next workshop, a shy Jamaican girl whispers to one of the seniors, "I never knew my grandma. Do you think she was like you?" It's a touching question and one that is particularly moving in view of the impact that immigration may have on the lives of these children. Sharing experiences and developing trusting relationships with the seniors is foremost for this group of third graders. They are not yet ready for recording their own activities, but need, instead, to talk with the seniors and listen to their stories.

In her discussion of current threats to childhood and their effects on education, Patricia Carini (1986) recalls the rapt response of a group of inner-city first graders to *The Little House in the Big Woods* by Laura Ingalls Wilder: "A narrative underscoring closeness, family, and cooperative work evoked for the children quieting and strengthening images such as that of the grandmother. Those images brought calm and restfulness. The stories also did what stories always do: they strengthened memory, identity, and a sense of place and belonging." Wilder's book struck a powerful chord in these children, Carini notes, not because the story was "relevant" to their own daily lives, but because it let them envision a possibility and gave form to their longing for deep roots and relatedness to others. The senior-child project seems to serve the same needs.

Once the seniors and the third graders have completed the warm-up exercises, Ms. D. reminds them of all the stories they've shared, about Trinidad, about Panama, and about the U.S. South. "How would you walk to Trinidad?" she asks. "How would you walk in hot weather?" She demonstrates. The kids and seniors follow her example.

Ms. D. shifts the scene to a cruise. A couple of boys pretend they are deep-sea fishing; several seniors take make-believe sunbaths. Others in the group play games. There is dialogue—about the beautiful weather, about catching a shark, and so on. Ms. D. points out that people let their bodies relax on a cruise. Next, the kids and seniors trade places, behaving as they think the others would behave. Seniors untie their shoelaces, remove their shoes, and shuffle around as they have seen kids do. One feigns a tantrum. "Freeze!" says Dawn. "Now, be yourselves." When each scene ends, she asks the audience to retell the sequence of actions in it. Once she asks a senior not to direct the children: "You become a character too. Don't direct them just because you're older."

The session ends in a unity circle, with everyone chanting in unison: "I am beautiful. I love myself. I love my eyes, my nose, my lips, my hands, my legs, my brain. I'm intelligent. I will do great things."

PUTTING IT ALL TOGETHER: FIFTH GRADERS AND SENIORS IN QUEENS

On a bitter cold February morning, the sidewalks leading from the top of Kissena Boulevard to the Self-Help Benjamin Rosenthal Senior Center are deserted. But in the center's auditorium four seniors—Vera and Stan Fogelman and Al Nachman and his brother Bob—are warmly greeting Chandrika Patel, Satya Sinha, Priscilla Kim, Zhen Dai, Lin Leung, and Rajat Sachdeva—fifth graders from P.S. 24. These East European Jewish elders and these Chinese, Korean, Indian, and Middle Eastern youngsters live in the same neighborhood and spend most of their days within a few blocks of one another. Without ESTA's living history project, however, they might never have met.

This morning, with Valentine's Day coming soon, some of the youngsters are giving handmade valentines to "their" seniors. Decorating the raised stage at the front of the auditorium, pink and red balloons float beside heart-shaped red mobiles. Bob, a tall senior with musical talent, climbs four steps up to the stage and walks to the right, ducking his head beneath the balloons. Several fifth graders follow. Taking a seat at an old piano, with the children clustered around him, he begins playing and singing "My Funny Valentine."

The kids and the seniors are about halfway through the development of their project. Since mid-December, apart from winter holidays, ESTA's Joanne Schultz has brought them together at the senior center for weekly workshops lasting an hour to an hour and a half. "Let's get started, you guys!" As soon as Schultz speaks, the energy in the room heightens. Children bring folding chairs from along the walls of the auditorium to the middle of the room, and arrange them in a semicircle large enough to accommodate themselves, their classmates, and the seniors. Susan Maloney, the fifth grade teacher, assists them. Twenty-eight fifth graders and ten seniors follow Schultz closely as she leads a series of warm-up exercises. Facing the group, she stands in the middle of the semicircle. Like soldiers, the children and adults stand at attention, eyes front, hands at their sides, waiting for her to give them marching orders.

"Shake it out!" Schultz shakes her arms above her head, out to her sides, and behind her back. "Shake it out!" She stamps her feet, claps her hands, dances a few steps to the rhythms she is clapping, and shouts, "What do you want to shake out?" "Money!" calls a fifth grader. "Oh, that's *good*!" Schultz responds delightedly. "School!" shouts another. The whole group joins in appreciative laughter.

"At first," Maloney relates, "when Joanne asked a question like 'What do you want to shake out?' none of the kids in my class would answer. They were trying to figure out the 'right' answer. Now, they've learned there is no right or wrong answer here. It's sharing your feelings and thoughts that's important."

Schultz underlines the classroom teacher's observations. "When kids attend the workshop as part of school, they tend to look at it as a class. For many, what matters most is the right answer—if you're not sure you have it, you keep your mouth shut. [....] But students need to move beyond trying to supply the correct answer in order to enter a process of sharing their opinions and feelings and engaging in meaningful conversations. This will put them on an equal footing with the seniors and promote greater trust among group members. It helps if the classroom teacher assists the teaching artist by discussing the difference between the group and a school class" (Schultz 1994: 43).

Indicating that the first part of the warm-up is over, Schultz takes a seat in the circle. "Send your name out," she instructs. And, one after another, the seniors and the children sit down, calling out their own names. From time to time, Schultz prompts someone: "Rajat, send your name all the way over to Mrs. Stanley." In the interplay, children and elders find a resonance in one another that strengthens their voices and their courage. The performance that Schultz and her colleagues are helping them create will amplify their voices and the truths they speak.

"Now, throw an imaginary ball and say the name of the person you're throwing it to," Schultz tells Chandrika. "Make eye contact as you pass the ball." Chandrika throws the ball to Vera Fogelman. Vera throws it to Zhen. Some people shout the names, hurling the ball across the circle; others speak softly and pass the ball to the person sitting next to them. When one of the seniors tosses the ball to Schultz, the exercise ends.

"*That* was an improvisation," explains Schultz. "You're given an instruction to do something, but *how* you do it is up to you." The next improvisation involves telephone conversations between pairs of fifth graders. Imaginary phones are passed around the circle. Influenced, perhaps, by the approach of Valentine's Day, two girls discuss whether or not one of them should kiss a boy she likes. "Can we make this a conference call?" interrupts Schultz, bringing one of the seniors into the conversation. "Vera, you come on the line with them." Soon Vera is giving the two girls suggestions for what gifts they might give their boyfriends on Valentine's Day.

Again Schultz emphasizes that the telephone callers are improvising. "Just talking. No script. Like the interview shows you practiced with each other in class, remember?" Next, she produces a microphone and she and the classroom teacher, with help from an ESTA intern, get the children into small groups to prepare for interview shows with the seniors. Reminding the kids that they must announce the names of their shows, introduce their guests properly, and conclude with thanks to the interviewees, Schultz launches the interview exercise.

The children have already talked informally with the seniors, exchanging memories and experiences on more than one occasion. These conversations provide the basis for the interview shows, which are improvised on the spot. The children who are chosen by the class to host a show pull their chairs to the front of the semicircle and invite a senior guest to be interviewed. With fanfare, Schultz introduces the show and the children begin the interview. The tone is relaxed. Shy children receive help and encouragement from Schultz, from their classroom teacher, or from the interviewees themselves. Everyone seems to enjoy the entertainment. Several youngsters conduct interviews that sound almost as professional as those on television. Here is Zhen, introducing Stanley:

Zhen: My first guest is—ta-da-da DUM-pa-PUM!!—STANLEY!
    (APPLAUSE). Stanley, I want to ask you, when you were little, you
    smoked your first cigar. Will you tell us about it?
Stanley: My father caught me smoking cigarettes. He said, "You wanna
    smoke? Come in here. I went into his room, where he worked, and took
    three puffs on a cigar. At first I wanted to do it. But then I nearly. . . . .
Zhen: Puked?
Stanley (laughing): Yes.
Zhen: How old were you then?
Stanley: I was ten years old.
Zhen: Are you married?
Stanley: Yes, for 47 years.
Zhen: And how did you meet this special person?

Taking evident pleasure in his skills, Zhen smoothly guides Stanley through the story of his romance and his wedding. As Stanley finishes the tale, Zhen invites him to share his memories of serving in World War II. But here Schultz stops them. Others want a turn. Anela and Valene interview Morris on what Schultz calls "a controversial topic," introducing a show called "Love at First Sight."

Anela: Hello, Morris. How old were you when you first kissed someone?
Morris: Eight or nine. At a party. We were playing Spin-the-Bottle.
Valene: Who did you kiss? What was her name? Or his?
Morris (disconcerted by Valene's casual acceptance of gender interchange):
    Frankly. . . . I've forgotten.
Anela: Are you married?
Morris: No.
Valene: Any children?
Morris: Yes. (He gives his children's names and ages.)
Anela: Where did you go when you dated girls?
Morris: First date? Movies.

Schultz brings the interview to a close, saying, "Well, we're having a real Valentine feast here today."

Al Nachman, who has been involved with ESTA's program in the schools for several years, is the next senior to be interviewed. An experienced interviewee, Al helps two shy boys get started.

Al: You wanna know how I earned my first dollar? Ask me how I earned my first dollar.
Boys: How did you earn your first dollar?
Al: Working at a silk house, where they sold silk, cotton, linen, wool. In those days a dollar was enough for everyone to go out and have something to eat—cake for five cents, coffee for five cents, movies for two and a half cents. Two people went to the movies for five cents. If you only had two cents, you'd stand outside the movie house and ask everyone who came along, "Anybody got three?" Until you found someone with three cents who'd go in with you.
Boys: Five cents? Two for five? (They shake their heads in disbelief.)

Love, war, money, challenging the rules: The interview shows touch on many issues of concern to these fifth graders. "Just one person who listens to a young person's opinions, concerns, and feelings without judging can create a lifeline to self-respect," says ESTA's Perlstein. "This is a traditional role of the grandparent: reassurance and support."

As the workshops progress, the youngsters discover that they and their families share remarkably similar stories with the seniors—stories of facing persecution and economic hardship in their original homelands and struggling to find their way as new Americans. The theme chosen for a senior-kid show is often related to the underlying quasi-ritual function that is served by the performance. In one instance, a group self-portrait emerged, showing that young and old, of many different ethnicities, all immigrants, were also all Americans. They belonged here; this was their home.

Gloria Wagner, Principal of P.S. 24 in Flushing, Queens, has worked at the school for nearly twenty years as a teacher and an administrator, and she is justifiably proud of the improvements that have taken place under her leadership. Known as the School of Authors and Illustrators, P.S. 24 includes nine hundred children in kindergarten through sixth grade. The population is so diverse that Wagner uses a special stamp when she has important messages to send home to the children's families. In Chinese, Korean, Arabic, and Spanish it says "Please have this translated immediately—very important!" A parent volunteer who grew up in India writes the same message, in one or more of the Indian languages, beneath the stamped one.

Despite the diversity of their backgrounds, Wagner sometimes feels the children are "living in a vacuum. They're shielded—even a child of ten or eleven has little or no concept of the community. Yes, they may go to church or to an after-school program in the neighborhood and they may have a strong family culture, but there's no *community* sense. That's why the elders prove to be one of the best influences on our kids. The children are able to identify with the seniors; they just mesh in some way." She says the fifth graders talk about the elders project constantly, at home and at school. Once, when they misbehaved with a substitute teacher, Wagner told them she was considering canceling their next workshop with the elders. They all wrote her letters, arguing that they were entitled to make one mistake and telling her they wanted to continue the elders project "more than anything."

To extend and complement the living history theater they are creating with the seniors, the fifth graders are also documenting their experience for a class anthology. With help from their classroom teacher, even newcomers to the English language write descriptions of "their" seniors that reveal a growing attachment to them (see Fig. 7-1 and 7-2).

Schultz sometimes wonders where to put the emphasis: Should it be on the issues that kids and seniors want to discuss, or on teaching them theater skills, or on putting together a show? In practice, she emphasizes all three at different times during the process. By April, she identifies a theme that draws together many of the issues under discussion among fifth graders and seniors in their weekly workshops: the theme of power. One morning she

Zhen Dai

Stanley

My senior is Stanley and he is 72 years old. He is a member at the Benjamin Rosenthal Senior Center. I found out that he was married, has children and grandchildren and the person he married to was in Benjamin Rosenthal Senior Center too!

When Stanley was 10, his father caught him smoking a cigarette. His father told him to go to his room. "You wants to smoke" okay" said his father as he took out a cigar "smoke this." Stanley took three puffs. He got an upset stomach and then, he ran in to bathroom and threw up.

Stanley also told us about his first kiss. When he was 12 he got his first kiss. He went on a date with a girl, she was pretty. The girl kissed him, and ask Stanley to go bike riding.

When Stanley was little, his father owned a store. It was a general store. Things were cheap, A broom was only $.19. Today we can not get a broom for just $.19.

Stanley was a very nice person. He was good to us. I hope I can learn more about him the next time we meet.

FIG. 7-1: Zhen and Stanley

JOHNNY GUEN

AL

My senior is AL. He is a senior citizen. We met him at the Benjamin Rosenthal Senior Center. AL is between the ages of 40-70. AL is very funny.

The first time AL got his first dollar is when it was his eleventh birthday. He spent it on ice cream and the movies. In the old days ice cream was 5 cents and so was the movies. The seniors are lucky, the food was so cheap in the old days. Now it is kind of expensive. I asked AL if he likes the Benjamin Rosenthal Senior Center. He said he really loves the senior center because it gives him a chance to meet with friends his own age and have someone to talk to and to listen to him. He is very exciting, very talkative and very interesting. I am looking forward to going there again.

FIG. 7-2: Johnny's Description of Al

asks the workshop participants to call out whatever words come to mind when they hear the word *power*. From the large number of responses, she constructs a tentative intergenerational "performance collage" on power.

In the remaining six to eight sessions, she directs the seniors and kids in a series of tableaux that dramatize the meanings of power. As they work together, dramatic, often humorous, scenes take shape. Some of the fifth grade girls invent a cheer about power and Schultz shows them how it can be used to provide continuity from one scene to another. One of the boys accompanies parts of the performance on African drums. In one scene, Chinese silk flags wave from bamboo poles as actors, portraying forces of nature, brandish them with powerful arm motions. The actors represent a mix of languages, nationalities, and generations; their living history theatre represents a mix of theatrical cultural traditions.

Introducing the performance to an audience of children and adults in the school auditorium, Schultz uses the same interactive techniques that she used with the fifth graders and the seniors during the weeks of preparation. "What do you think of when you hear the word *power*?" she asks. Students in the audience respond: "full of strength," "in complete control," "do anything you want." "You can use power in many different ways," Schultz tells them. "See if you agree or disagree with our ideas. We're going to save twenty-five minutes after the show for comments from the audience." Then she asks the members of the audience to raise their hands if they have ever made a collage. Several students say they have and, on being asked, someone describes it as a collection of "odds and ends—pictures of cars, people, animals." Schultz tells the audience that the performance they are going to see is "a collage that comes to life—a collage of colors, sounds, and words—made out of all the stories we've heard."

The fifth grade teacher takes her place among the students onstage, the boy on drums starts a dazzling solo, and cheerleaders march onto the stage chanting, "Pump up the power! Pump up the power!" The performance has begun. Schultz remains in the wings, unobtrusively guiding the players. At the end of each scene, she swings a tightly coiled, red plastic tube around her head; it makes a mysterious whirring sound, intended to represent the sound made by the *churinga* during an Australian aboriginal initiation rite, when the tribal elders celebrate the coming-of-age of the youths.

The brief period of audience participation led by Schultz follows the performance. The interaction between performers and spectators indicates that the performance, to say nothing of the many weeks of exercises that preceded it, has succeeded in diminishing stereotypes of age and ethnicity. Students in the audience are clearly impressed by the seniors' energy, humor, and willingness to "ham it up" with the fifth graders. The seniors, in turn, express their admiration for the fifth graders' talents and hard work.

Following theater tradition, the children give flowers to various adults involved in the production as a gesture acknowledging all the work they have done. Refreshments are served afterward, providing another way to celebrate the achievement and another opportunity for seniors and younger people to mix.

Children learn valuable new skills and enjoy the opportunity to demonstrate their talents in a living history theater project. The same goals may be met, however, by less ambitious approaches than the one described here. Other ideas for making a living history performance include *reader's theatre*, in which performers read/act their parts seated on stage, with scripts in hand. The positions of their chairs may suggest relationships between characters and may be changed from scene to scene. *Pageantry/spectacle* works well with large groups because it can include many people, as opposed to a scene with three or four characters. For example, half a dozen children waved colored silk flags at one point in the performance described above, suggesting natural forces such as wind, water, and fire, while simultaneously other children described the concepts of power associated with them, using a choral reading style. *Multimedia performed text* uses slides with accompanying spoken text. This technique was used by third graders in the immigration project described in Chapter 6.

In addition to (or instead of) the single performance, other types of presentations can celebrate a project. Intergenerational exercises have inspired murals of family trees. Words and images have been combined in booklet projects, with text superimposed on drawings or placed next to them. A video can be produced to record the oral history, interviewing phase of the program.

Teachers may wish to research these suggestions further at a library. Most can readily be adapted to meet a range of needs. But, no matter how simple or elaborate the project, the process itself must matter much more to the participants than the glamour of the results.

8

Family Album

*Through photography each family
constructs a portrait of itself, a kit
of images that bears witness to its
connectedness.*

—*Susan Sontag*

Whether they are framed and grouped on a table, arranged in an album, tossed into a desk drawer, taped to the outside of the refrigerator, or piled in a shoebox, family photographs document the important events in a family's life. When Steven Zeitlin and his colleagues studied thousands of American family photos they collected during the Smithsonian Folklife Festival in Washington, D.C., they found that certain categories emerged. "Scenes of holiday celebrations, birthdays, picnics, and vacations dominate these collections, and children, from infancy through high school graduation, are favorite subjects for the home photographer" (Zeitlin et al. 1982:182).

During the three years I spent doing ethnographic fieldwork in the Haitian-American community in New York City, (see Gutwirth-Winston 1988), I noticed that personal photograph albums, begun by adults in the family while the children were still infants, were entrusted to the children themselves from about the age of eight. While I was still a fairly new acquaintance of theirs, the children in the families I ultimately knew best often invited me to look through their albums with them while they described, lovingly and in detail, the people in the photographs and their relationships to their extended family. To my surprise, I eventually came upon photographs of me in these albums. I became aware then of the extent to which each album was indeed an inventory of its owner's ongoing, extended family and its ritual kinship relations. Shortly afterward, several of my Haitian friends who were struggling to make a living decided to pool their resources in order to buy a video camera so that videotapes could be added to their photographic records of family life.

Taking pictures and leafing through photo albums are often important aspects of family gatherings, but not all families take and display snapshots of shared experiences. Some families are averse to taking pictures and object even to having their children photographed for the annual class picture. As with every aspect of the family stories curriculum, teachers who wish to use student photographs need to show sensitivity to the variations in accepting such photos across families and cultural groups.

Photographs can bring to mind painful losses, and this may account for why some families choose not to show them. Zeitlin writes about a Jewish Holocaust survivor whose family did not show her the photos they brought with them from Germany until forty years after they had fled. Photographs are so powerful in eliciting family history, however, that their inclusion in the family stories curriculum seems warranted, provided appropriate care is taken for the feelings, traditions, and beliefs of all concerned. Where photographs do not exist or cannot be shared, other forms of memorabilia, such as original drawings or collages of magazine photos, may take their place so that all children who wish to create a family album may do so.

"Consciously or not," Zeitlin reminds us, "we tend to take photos according to the way we want to preserve, remember and be remembered." Although the image in a photograph is fixed, our interpretations of it can change—just as stories about our forebears may change, depending on the outlook of the viewer or teller. This is what makes photographs a rich storehouse of information about a family's evolving history, values, and ideals.

Two approaches to using photography in family studies are described here. The first draws on the work of Beth Maloney, who created a curriculum she calls "Reading Photos; Familial Relations" during her Bank Street College internship at the Lower East Side Tenement Museum in New York. The second, known as "Photo-Autobiography," was designed by a team of fifth grade teachers at Academy Elementary School in Madison, Connecticut.

READING PHOTOS; FAMILIAL RELATIONS

As an intern at the Village Community School, Beth Maloney brought a class of fifth grade students to visit the Lower East Side Tenement Museum, with the goal of exploring the environments of those who lived in that neighborhood at the turn of the century. More specifically, she wanted the students to explore definitions of families "as groups of people living and/or working together and sharing resources and responsibilities." The museum's tenement building depicts the lives of former residents, using material culture, urban archaeology, archival materials, oral histories, and photographs. To show fifth graders how material objects can trigger memories and, more specifically, how photographs are useful historical documents, Maloney began by bringing in some of her own photos from an album she compiled with her mother as a going-away-to-college keepsake. Without mentioning that they were her own family photographs, she presented them to the students, starting with one taken of her grandparents working together as scientists in their laboratory. She then asked the youngsters what they could guess from the photograph about the couple's relationship to each other. Were they coworkers, or relatives, or both? Next, Maloney showed pictures of herself as a baby and young child. Asking the fifth graders to "tell stories about the pictures" yielded guesses about the child's life and social background. A picture of young Beth on St. Patrick's Day, for example, led some students to suggest, "Maybe she's Irish." The photos stimulated many intriguing questions that the children could not answer. Who is the woman with that child? Is she the mother? An older sister? What did the expression on that boy's face mean? And what about the dog that's in so many of the pictures? Is it the girl's dog, or the photographer's dog?

By the time the girl in the photographs reached approximately the same age as the fifth graders, some of them suspected that they were pictures of Maloney. When they saw her high school prom picture, they knew for sure it was she. The last picture the kids looked at was one that brought past and present together in a single dramatic moment. Taken at her college graduation, it shows Maloney in a flowered dress with a gold locket around her neck—the very same dress and locket she was wearing as she and the students studied the photographs from her album! The locket contained pictures of her maternal grandparents.

Together, Maloney and the children asked and discussed, "What was there in the photographs that made us guess certain things about the people in them?" They posted Maloney's collection of pictures on a time line of her life, from birth to the present. The next day some of the kids spontaneously brought in their own photographs. Others followed suit. Without fanfare, each time one of the fifth graders brought in a photograph that fit somewhere on Maloney's time line, she put it there in place of her own. The classroom teacher also brought in her own photographs and arranged them on another timeline, one that reached back many more years than Maloney's did. As the children began bringing in even older photographs, of grandparents and great-grandparents, the time lines reached back further than Maloney had anticipated.

Inspired by the fifth graders' enthusiasm for working with photographs, Maloney developed a program that encourages her students who visit the Tenement Museum to think about how the past is uncovered and interpreted by examining copies of photographs taken on the Lower East Side by Jacob Riis, renowned social activist of the 1890s.

Maloney divided the students into small working groups of two or three and invited them to choose one photograph from a collection that she had mounted on foam core and spread out on a table. It is, of course, also possible for a teacher to distribute the photographs to the children; each strategy has its advantages, depending on the situation. Maloney asked her class, "Is there a difference between looking at a photograph and reading a photograph?" After giving the students time to look at their pictures carefully for three minutes, she then asked them to turn the pictures over, talk about them in relation to the following set of questions, and then jot down their answers: What is the historical context? What are the people doing? What is their relationship? Are they relatives? After the groups had discussed these questions and noted their answers, Maloney asked them to look at the photographs again, with new questions in mind: What aspects of the photograph were easiest to remember? What looks different now? What do you notice now? Again, discussion followed.

As a third step, Maloney distributed additional lists of questions to the groups, instructing them to examine and discuss their pictures again, guided by this latest questionnaire.

- Come up with several adjectives/descriptive phrases that explain the mood or feeling of the photograph.
- Take a look at where the photograph was taken. What might be the relationship between the people in the photograph?
- Does this photograph remind you of your family, or not at all? Why and how?
- Put yourself in the photograph. Where would you like to be and why?

Students discussed these questions in small groups for ten minutes. Since her aim was to raise questions about the relationships among people, Maloney chose photographs with two or more people in them. Some showed adults and young children working side by side at home; families were often coworkers as well as relatives. But Maloney did not mention this facet of Lower East Side turn-of-the-century life. She even covered the titles of the photographs so that the students were free to use their imaginations about the people in them. Her focus was not on the intent of the photographer but, rather, on what the students were seeing in the pictures. What messages did the children find in them? Families were working together. There were "families" without parents: Children, sleeping outdoors, were probably taking care of each other because they had no one else. Can a gang of teenaged youths living under a pier be a "family," not biologically related but still "brothers"? The questions helped the children slow down and pay careful attention to each picture. Bombarded with images since early childhood, they were, perhaps for the first time, learning to "read" a photograph as they might read a printed text.

The students analyzed the photos as they wished, in no particular order. One shows a family of seven gathered in a crowded tenement room in 1910. "I wouldn't want to be there; I'd rather be outside" was one of the responses elicited by the picture. Another photograph in which a young girl—maybe ten or eleven years old—is holding a baby on her lap brought these questions and comments: "Is she the mom?" "Is she the older sister?" "She looks older than she is because she has a lot of responsibilities." The last comment triggered a connection for some of the students, who had friends who were major caregivers for younger siblings.

A third photo, in which seven children are seated with a woman at a table making artificial flowers, raised different kinds of questions in the students' minds. Are the children all hers? Are some of them related to her, or to each other? Maybe the children are coworkers, employed by the woman? Are they doing homework? If not, why aren't they in school? (See Fig. 8-1).

Next, all the students gathered in a circle and those who wished to introduced their photograph to the whole class, speaking to the questions they had considered. Maloney encouraged discussion, sometimes posing more questions. The class then made generalizations, based on their answers, in the form of sentences that synthesized what they had learned from examining the photographs. Maloney then helped them make connections between their generalizations and the historical context of the photographs. Finally, she offered biographical information about Jacob Riis and social reform movements, which led to a discussion about what nineteenth-century social reformists saw as "healthy" environments for children and families.

A wrap-up discussion addressed further questions: Who would find reading photographs useful? What do photographs offer us for our research of the past? What do these photographs tell us about people and the places where they worked and lived? What do the photographs tell you about the way people related to each other? What were your first impressions of the photograph itself, the persons or objects in the photograph, the setting or the space, your feelings? How did the photographs convey a message without words?

Each student received a copy of a Riis photograph they had not yet seen to take it away as a stimulus to repeat these exercises in the classroom. They

FIG. 8-1: Around the Table

could also examine, interpret, and compare photos of their own families as a prelude to sharing their family histories.

PHOTO-AUTOBIOGRAPHY

Photo-autobiographies by fifth graders at Academy Elementary School are in the best sense, extensions of the facial masks made by the seven- and eight-year-olds at Manhattan Country School, described in Chapter 1. Based on careful observation by each child of his or her own close family, the photo-autobiographies are self-portraits that illuminate each child's life in the context of family culture and family history.

Sparked by a curriculum that centers on immigration like the one described in Chapter 6, photo-autobiography grew out of a project in which fifth graders choose an ancestor (or a surrogate), learn as much as they can about that person's character and life history, and then write the story of his or her journey to the United States. Later, dressed in the style of clothing their immigrant forebears might have worn, students enact their stories in dramatic monologues as a highlight of the celebration that concludes the immigration study. Typically, the youngsters bring photographs and other family keepsakes to accompany the monologues, sharing them with school-mates and adult visitors who come to hear the immigrant stories and talk with the children who tell them.

At the outset of the project, which lasts from November to May, teachers ask all fifth graders to read parts of Russell Freedman's *Lincoln: A Photobiography* as an introduction to the genre. Other Freedman books on Franklin Delano Roosevelt, on the Wright brothers, and on immigrant kids serve as models of photobiography. Photo-autobiographies created by pre-vious fifth graders also provide examples of what might be appropriately included.

Fifth grade teachers put together a packet of guidelines for students and their families as research on their ancestors begins. It includes suggestions on how to look at and interpret photographs, since photos are often effective props for eliciting information from a recalcitrant family member who insists, "I don't have anything to talk about." Also included in the packet of guidelines are sample lists of interview questions for parents and grand-parents. Drawn from many published guides for gathering oral histories, they cover such topics as family members' countries of origin, early years in America, schools, neighborhoods, work places, favorite activities, courtships, marriages, houses and household routines, children's births, family names, collections, pets, and games. Before interviewing their fami-lies, the fifth graders try out their questionnaires in interviews with elderly residents of a nursing home near their school.

Once a week, as the study evolves, the children gather in small groups or as a whole class to share the stories and artifacts they are considering for inclusion in their photo-autobiographies. On one occasion, grandparents come to the weekly meeting with an album containing photographs of the ship that brought them to America. At another meeting, a girl talks about how she clutched her father's shoulders as they swam across the Rio Grande from Guatemala. Her teacher gives her a copy of *Journey of the Sparrows*, a book about a family from El Salvador who had also crossed the Rio Grande to get to the United States. After she and her older sister read the book, they read it aloud to the rest of the family, translating from English to Spanish so their parents can share the story with them.

Fifth grade teachers work as a team during the project. One leads the brainstorming sessions that prepare students to begin writing their own photo-autobiographies. Another works with them on photo analysis. A third helps in making maps, locating the countries, towns, and villages of the

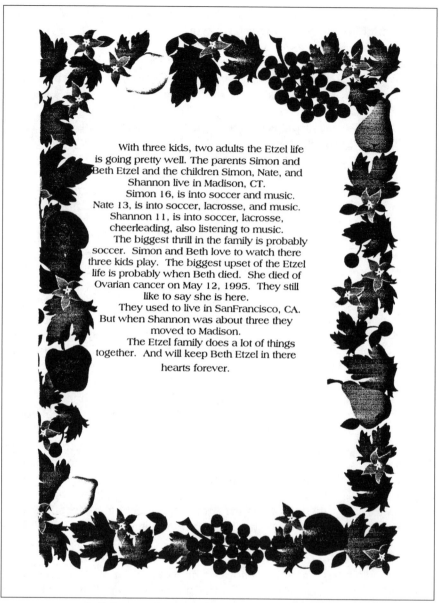

With three kids, two adults the Etzel life is going pretty well. The parents Simon and Beth Etzel and the children Simon, Nate, and Shannon live in Madison, CT.

Simon 16, is into soccer and music. Nate 13, is into soccer, lacrosse, and music. Shannon 11, is into soccer, lacrosse, cheerleading, also listening to music.

The biggest thrill in the family is probably soccer. Simon and Beth love to watch there three kids play. The biggest upset of the Etzel life is probably when Beth died. She died of Ovarian cancer on May 12, 1995. They still like to say she is here.

They used to live in SanFrancisco, CA. But when Shannon was about three they moved to Madison.

The Etzel family does a lot of things together. And will keep Beth Etzel in there hearts forever.

FIG. 8-2: Shannon's Memorial to Her Mother

TRADITIONS

Holiday Traditions

My family and I always go to my Grandma & Grandpa Ford's house in Bethany, Connecticut. It is always a lot of fun.

There is always raw shrimp with a red sauce on the table before eating, and only the adults eat it. This year, I tried it, but didn't like it. A dip with vegetables is always there also. I'm the only one who really eats it.

There is always a KID Table and a GROWN-UP Table. My cousins and I wish we could someday sit at the GROWN-UP Table.

At the KID Table, there is always a baby game we play called "Bad Woof." The way we play goes like this: we pretend that there is a mad dog under the table trying to bite us. So we put our feet up on our chairs. I call this game "The Little Ford Legend." It all started when my cousins and I were outside and heard a ferocious barking from a house about a mile away.

When I first get there and I walk into the house, my grandpa is always watching something on TV. Then, after what I like to call "Lupper," I sit down and talk to him. Then I watch football.

"No Applause"

Feel embarrassed about something? Well what if it happened every beginning of each year for your entire life? That's what I used to go through every January 13!

I will never allow anyone to clap after singing the birthday song to me. There is something about me that makes me feel so embarrassed, you can't imagine how bad it is.

ANCESTORS

"Wars"

Fire and bullets are being spread over the land below. Thomas Ford, flying over France carrying supplies is nervous. Bullets are shot at him but he flies on in World War II.

Dr. Gabriel Cusano has a totally different job, but is in the same war. He is the Navy's dentist. You may think it's silly, but if you were fighting and got a horrible tooth ache, you'd be thankful for him when he would fix it if you would be able to go back and fight.

These two men are my grandfathers. My second cousin, Joe Fahey, fought in the Vietnam War. He had no training at all because he was drafted by the Army.

FIG. 8-3: Holiday Traditions and War Stories

youngsters' ancestors, as well as their routes to America. A fourth teaches Neil Diamond's song, "Coming to America", and others supervise art projects, such as designing and making a family crest inscribed with a family motto.

Despite the popularity of the project, there are pitfalls. At first, some children may be distressed by the assignment, convinced that they have nothing of interest to put into a photo-autobiography. But teachers should urge them to stick with the process, invariably, the students discover that they and their families are much more interesting than they had imagined. "The kids don't realize what their heritage is until they start doing the research," one teacher says. Even a family tragedy, such as the death of a beloved parent, makes the photo-autobiography an especially valuable if, perhaps, poignant exercise for a child (see Fig. 8-2).

As a marriage of photographs and text, each photo-autobiography is a unique expression of the author's personality. However, the children tend to adopt similar formats, dividing their books into chapters with titles such as

The Beginning, School Days, Family Traditions, Family Treasures, Ancestors, Special Interests, Friends, Pets, and Dreams. One youngster wrote that his photo-autobiography "will be an important heirloom for my family for generations and generations to come."

Holiday traditions and stories of wartime service are also important memories (see Fig. 8-3). Likewise, information about events such as births, marriages, and deaths, recorded in a family Bible, may be included in a photo-autobiography. A picture of great-great-great-grandmother leads to a reflection on family resemblances. As one child noted, "You can sort of compare some of her features to my dad."

A family's wedding photographs can show striking differences across generations. Laura Benevento's photo-autobiography contains a photo of her great-grandparents' wedding, in which the dominating patriarchal figure of her great-great-grandfather takes center stage. He is standing between his daughter and her groom. Bride and groom are seated next to their attendants. Two small children—from the youngest generation of the family—sit side by side directly in front of him. No one smiles (see Fig. 8-4).

FIG. 8-4: Wedding Photograph

A generation later, in the same family, a wedding photograph shows a smiling, relaxed bride and groom standing side by side, flanked by their maid of honor and best man, with no others present.

All the photo-autobiographies are placed on exhibit in the school gymnasium during the fifth graders' annual Coming to America Day. During the following week, the students devote a daily class period to reading each other's books and writing comments on a separate page reserved for that purpose at the back of each book. As children look over one another's photographs, they appreciate more fully parents and children and grandchildren who have grown up, and grown old, and died, bringing generations past, present, and future into closer touch. Photographs thus give children an initial understanding of generational depth, a concept that tends to interest them even at an early age.

9
Epilogue

*We live our lives like chips in a kaleidoscope, always part
of patterns that are larger than ourselves and somehow
more than the sum of their parts.*

—*Salvador Minuchin in "Family Kaleidoscope".*

I began this book with the intention of naming and celebrating family stories as a curricular theme. Now, reaching the end, surrounded by echoes of the voices of children and adults who told their family stories in the classrooms I observed, I want to celebrate the storytellers themselves. They affirm that our lives and memories are interwoven in patterns, which go beyond the individual.

My experience in exchanging stories with colleagues suggests that family stories can help teachers learn naturally and spontaneously about the diverse cultures of the children in their classrooms. I have tried in these pages to suggest how the family stories approach fits an anthropologist's definition of relationship as knowledge, achieved and sustained through conversation and information exchange (Bateson 1984: 230).

As the research of linguists and anthroplogists has shown (Heath 1982, 1983, 1986; Miller, Fung, and Mintz 1991; Ochs and Schieffelin 1984; Schieffelin and Ochs 1986), cultures shape the uses of stories in multiple ways across the ages and situations of the tellers and their listeners. Studies indicate that by the time children enter kindergarten, they have experienced several years of personal storytelling, both as listeners and as narrators. Such storytelling is an important means through which young children, together with their family members, experience self in relation to other (Miller and Mehler 1991:47). When children move from the family into school, they face a new task of understanding themselves in relation to their teachers and fellow students, and integrating who they are at home with who they are at school.

Recounting personal experiences is only one approach to getting children off to a good start in school. Unless teachers are sensitive to, and respectful of, variation in styles of discourse that children bring from home (Michaels 1981, 1986), merely encouraging such talk has as much potential for undermining as for supporting self-esteem. But sharing personal experience stories in school clearly seems to be important to the process of self-development for children (Paley 1990, 1992).

There is much variation in the amount of time given to incorporating personal experience stories into classroom talk and, not surprisingly, variation in frequency tends to be related to class size, with personal narrative occurring most often where teacher-pupil ratios are comparatively low. Although children are encouraged to report on experiences outside the classroom during sharing time (Cazden 1991; Michaels 1981, 1986), it is talk about personal experience, rather than personal storytelling, that seems to occur in most classrooms. Very few personal stories—either by the teacher or the children—seem to be as complex as those told in homes, and almost none seem to be as fully performed (Tizard and Hughes 1984; Wells 1986). These chapters contain many examples of how using family stories in classrooms can help decrease this home-school disparity.

As I consider what makes family stories an effective teaching resource in the classrooms described here, the first thing that comes to mind is not storytelling but, rather, listening. Learning to listen to each other's stories with an open mind and heart is the recurring refrain that ties together the different approaches to family stories presented in these pages. Families in a storytelling workshop listen to the workshop coordinator as she tells one story after another, until at last they can no longer resist telling their own stories, gathering them from others, sharing them in their children's classrooms, and, eventually, publishing anthologies. One parent writes this moving introduction to *The Speaking Forest* (1996: 7), an anthology of family stories gathered and published by families at his child's school: "Hearing stories, we learn to be ourselves; the forward rush of these tales gives us a way to shape our recollections. The telling of stories and the sharing of the past are modes of communication, as deep as touch, and the narratives themselves, passed along in their ever changing shapes, link us to all the generations that preceded us on this earth and to all the ones that are yet to come."

In rapt attention, first graders in Chinatown listen as their teachers and other adults on the school staff tell family stories in the classroom. Soon the children and their characteristically reticent families respond to the teachers' stories by sharing their own. Similarly, teachers' initiatives in the poetry and memoir projects described here prompt children's (and their families') eagerness to participate.

When teachers listen compassionately, they respond with comments and questions that allow the moral implications of a young child's story to emerge, rather than being imposed on it. This fosters the child's sense of empathy, deepening the connections among children, their teachers, and their families. The power of such listening is reflected in a poignant entry from a dialogue journal one third grader in an inner-city school kept with his teacher: "I was afraid that mother is going to die, but she didn't die and I was happy and proud of myself and when she came home it was her birthday and I speprail [surprise] her and give her gifts and she went to sleep, thank you for listen" (Mosle 1995:60).

I set out to highlight the work of teachers who are mindful of the ideological snares that lie beneath concepts like "family" and "family values." I wanted readers to question conventional notions of family and discard the myths that inhibit our ability to see the complexities of family life. In several chapters, diverse groups of children, guided by their teachers, tackle the question of how to define "family" by gathering, reflecting on, and sharing information from their own families. Students in Brooklyn and Queens exchange family stories with senior citizens in the neighborhoods surrounding their schools, and then develop surrogate grandparent-grandchild relationships as they work with "their" seniors to produce dramatizations of their stories. This is one example of how "family" may be redefined to include neighbors who were once strangers to one another.

Several chapters reveal the role of family stories in giving children a sense of history and a connection with the past. A grandparent's letter tells what life was like when he was a child. An adult's account of being an immigrant portrays the courage needed to make a new life in a new land. A senior citizen's description of his military service makes World War II come alive. Family photographs and other memorabilia create a kind of living history that captures children's imaginations.

Although there is evidence of cultural learning in every chapter, Chapter 5 provides the most direct and immediate example. When home cooking comes to school, teachers and children gain insights into cultural differences and similarities in both concrete and abstract ways through the smells, tastes, textures, and sights of foods as basic as breads and soups and through metaphors, proverbs, and stories associated with cooking and food. Sharing a cooking project with their families, children develop skills in sorting, counting, adding, subtracting, multiplying, dividing, problem solving, and basic chemistry. Making a class cookbook based on family recipes gives the children practice in writing a "how-to" book.

The contribution of family stories to the development of children's creativity and their confidence in their academic skills informs each of the chapters. As primary sources, families provide occasions for young children to learn basic research skills, such as interviewing and recording information from interviews. Several chapters offer examples of this process as children at different grade levels engage in research that results in profiles of significant adults in their lives. They also learn to transform information from family interviews into puppetry, museum displays, and living history theater. As they explore the social and historical implications of family photographs, children begin to contextualize their own experiences within the wider worlds of the extended family and community.

Stories and storytelling are clearly linked to the development of literacy. Through listening to stories and through telling them, children learn sequencing and structure. They also begin to appreciate the sensual and metaphoric properties of language: the rhythms, rhymes, figures of speech, and dialogic voices that communicate feelings. Whether they participate in a classroom poetry project, a memoir study, or another aspect of the curriculum, families in all the chapters are major sources of their children's literacy.

Picture books support the family stories curriculum in every classroom described, giving children opportunities to read independently and in small groups, as well as to hear teachers and family members read aloud. Reading and discussing picture books with immigration themes, in which the central characters are approximately the same ages as the children reading about them, personalizes the abstract process of immigration for third graders and helps them identify with the immigration stories they are gathering from adults in family research interviews. Participants in family storytelling workshops learn to make picture books based on their own experiences. Those that have age-appropriate themes can be shared with their children. The annotated bibliography that follows this chapter includes picture books that teachers have found useful as windows through which children can see "real-life families" that sometimes resemble and sometimes differ from their own.

My purpose in writing this book was to portray the process and results of bringing family stories into elementary classrooms in ways that might encourage readers to take off on their own. All the approaches depicted in these pages can be used in most elementary classrooms. Each can be modified to suit different conditions, adapted for children at various grade levels,

and used in combination with others. The flexibility of the family stories curriculum is its chief strength, the source of its enduring power. The most
important attributes of the teachers leading family stories programs are
enthusiasm, friendliness, and an ability to keep people at ease and focussed
on active listening. An effective leader will create a "safe" setting in which all
the children, their families, and their teachers recognize that sharing family
stories is a communal event and that every story is special.

Works Cited

Applebee, A. 1993. *Beyond the lesson: Restructuring Curriculum as a Domain for Culturally Significant Conversations*. Report Series 1.7. Albany, New York: National Research Center on Literature, Teaching and Learning.

Bateson, M.C. 1984. *With A Daughter's Eye*. New York: William Morrow.

Bruner, J. 1986. *Actual Minds, Possible Worlds*. Cambridge, MA: Harvard University Press.

———.1990. *Acts of Meaning*. Cambridge, MA: Harvard University Press.

Calkins, L.M. 1982. *Lessons from a Child: On the Teaching and Learning of Writing*. Portsmouth, NH: Heinemann.

———.1996. *Keynote Address*. The Writing Project, Teachers College of Columbia University (Spring).

Calkins, L.M. and S. Harwayne. 1991. *Living Between the Lines*. Portsmouth, NH: Heineman Educational Books.

Carini, P.F. 1986. "Building from Children's Strengths." *Journal of Education* (168): 13–24.

Casper, V., S. Schultz, and E. Wickens. 1992. "Breaking the Silences: Lesbian and Gay Parents and the Schools." In *Teachers College Record* 94: 109–137.

Cazden, C.B. 1994. "What is Sharing Time For?" In *The Need for Story: Cultural Diversity in Classroom and Community*, eds. A.H. Dyson and C. Genishi, 72–79 Urbana, IL: National Council of Teachers of English.

Cheung, D. No date. "The Tao of Learning: Socialization of Chinese American children." Unpublished doctoral dissertation, Stanford University. Cited in Heath, S.B., 1986a (see reference below).

Cisneros, S. 1991 *The House on Mango Street*. New York: Random House.

Crimmins, P. 1996. *Introduction: The Speaking Forest*. New York: Children's Workshop School.

Daigen, L. No date. *Nuestro Mundo: A Multicultural Core Curriculum for seven- and eight-year-olds*. Unpublished Master's Thesis, T 1984 D 132 N. New York: Bank Street College of Education.

Dillard, A. 1988. *An American Childhood*. New York: Harper Collins.

Dyson, A.H. and C. Genishi. 1994. *The Need for Story: Cultural Diversity in Classroom and Community*. Urbana, IL: National Council of Teachers of English.

Farrell, C. 1991. *Storytelling: A Guide for Teachers*. New York: Scholastic.

Freedman, R. 1987. *Lincoln: A Photobiography*. New York: Houghton Mifflin.

Freire, P. 1973. *Education for Critical Consciousness*. New York: Seabury Press.

Greenfield, E. and L.J. Little. 1993. Childtimes: *A Three-Generation Memoir*. New York: HarperTrophy.

Gutwirth, V. 1997. "A Multicultural Family Study Project for Primary." *Young Children* 52 (2): 74–81

Gutwirth-Winston, L. 1988, "Domestic and Kinship Networks of Some American Born Children of Haitian Immigrants." In *Social Networks of Children, Adolescents and College Students*, eds. S. Salzinger, J. Antrobus, and M. Hammer, 263–284. Hillsdale, NJ: Lawrence Erlbaum Associates.

Heard, G. 1989. *For the Good of the Earth and Sun*. Portsmouth, NH: Heinemann.

Heath, S.B. 1982. "What No Bedtime Story Means: Narrative skills at home and school." *Language in Society* (II): 49–76.

——— . 1983. *Ways with Words: Language, Life and Work in Communities and Classrooms*. New York: Cambridge University Press.

——— . 1986a. "Taking a Cross-Cultural Look at Narratives." *Topics in Language Disorders*. 7 (1): 84–94.

——— . 1986b. "The Book as Narrative Prop in Language Acquisition." In *The Acquisition of Literacy: Ethnographic Perspectives*, eds., B.B. Schieffelin and P. Gilmore, 16–34. New Jersey: Ablex.

Kingston, M.H. 1989. *The Woman Warrior*. New York: Random House.

Krogness, M.M. 1987. "Folklore: A Matter of the Heart and the Heart of the Matter." *Language Arts* 64 (8): 809–818.

——— . 1994. *Just Teach Me, Mrs. K*. Portsmouth, NH: Heinemann.

Lewis, D.S. and G. Lewis. 1994. *Did I Ever Tell You About When You Were Little?* Grand Rapids, MI: Zondervan Publishing House.

Martin, D. 1991. "Giving Children Roots and Wings with Stories: It's Confabulating." *New York Times*, April.

McEwen, C. 1995. "Mrs. Rainey's Grandma." In *Old Faithful: 18 Writers Present Their Favorite Writing Assignments*, eds. C. Edgar and R. Padgett, 136–143. New York: Teachers and Writers Collaborative.

Michaels, S. 1981. "Sharing Time: Children's narrative styles and differential access to literacy." *Language in Society* (10): 423–442.

———. 1986. "Narrative Presentations: An oral preparation for literacy with first graders." In *The Social Construction of Literacy*, ed. J. Cook-Gumperz, 94–116. New York: Cambridge University Press.

Miller, P.J., H. Fung, and J. Mintz. 1991, October. *Creating Children's Selves in Relational Contexts: A comparison of American and Chinese narrative practices.* Paper presented at the meeting of Society for Psychological Anthropology, Chicago.

Miller, P.J. and R.A. Mehler. 1994. "The Power of Personal Storytelling in Families and Kindergartens." *In The Need for Story*, eds. A.H. Dyson and C. Genishi, 38–54.

Minuchin, S. 1984. *Family Kaleidoscope*. Cambridge, MA: Harvard University Press.

Morgan, K.L. 1976. "Caddy buffers: Legends of a middle-class black family in Philadelphia." In *Festival of American Folklife*, ed. B.H. Lomax. Washington, DC: Smithsonian.

———. 1980. *Children of Strangers: The Stories of a Black Family*. Philadelphia, PA: Temple University Press.

Mosle, S. 1995. "Writing Down Secrets." *The New Yorker* (Annals of Childhood). September 18: 52–61.

Ochs, E. and B.B. Schieffelin. 1984. "Language Acquisition and Socialization: Three developmental stories and their implications." In *Culture Theory*, eds. R.A. Shweder and R.A. LeVine, 276–320.

Paley, V.G. 1990. *The Boy Who Would Be a Helicopter: The Uses of Storytelling in the Classroom*. Cambridge, MA: Harvard University Press.

———. 1992. *You Can't Say You Can't Play*. Cambridge, MA: Harvard University Press.

Perlstein, S. and J. Bliss. 1994. *Generating Community: Intergenerational Partnerships Through the Expressive Arts*. New York: Elders Share the Arts.

Roberts, J. 1994. *Tales & Transformations: Stories in Families and Family Therapy*. New York: Norton Press.

Rosen, H. 1988. "The Irrepressible Genre." In *Oracy Matters: The development of talking and listening in education*, eds. M. Maclure, T. Phillips, and A. Wilkinson, 13–23. Philadelphia: Open Press.

Savage, M.C. 1993. "Give a Story/Get a Story." in *Parents Have Stories to Tell: Stories to Support Home and School Literacy Development*. New York: Henry Street Settlement Arts in Education Program.

———. 1992. "Parents Have Stories to Tell." Presentation to NCTE Postconference Workshop in Culture-based Teaching. Seattle, WA (October).

———. (in press). *Seed Stories for Multicultural Times*. In *Teaching for Change*. Washington, DC: Network of Educators on the Americas.

Schieffelin, B.B. and E. Ochs. 1986. "Language Socialization." In *Annual Review of Anthropology*, ed. B. Siegel, 163–191. Palo Alto, CA: Annual Reviews.

Schiller, L. 1996. "Coming to America: Community from Diversity." *Language Arts* 73: 46–51.

Schwartz, P. 1995. "The Silent Family: Together but Apart." *The New York Times*. C6.

Simons, E.R. 1990. *Student Worlds, Student Words: Teaching Writing Through Folklore*. Portsmouth, NH: Boynton/Cook.

Sontag, S. 1977. *On Photography*. New York: Farrar, Strauss and Giroux.

Tan, A. 1989. *The Joy Luck Club*. New York: Vintage Books/Random House.

Taylor, D. 1983. *Family Literacy: Young Children Learning to Read and Write*. Portsmouth, NH: Heinemann.

Tizard, B. and M. Hughes. 1984. *Young Children Learning*. Cambridge, MA: Harvard University Press.

Trowbridge, A. 1993. "Being Sewn Together: Seven- and Eight-year-olds Study Their Families." In *Manhattan Country School Sampler* (1) 1: 1–3.

Vascellaro, S. and C. Genishi. 1994. "All the Things That Mattered: Stories Written by Teachers for Children." In *The Need for Story*, eds. A.H. Dyson and C. Genishi. Urbana, IL: National Council of Teachers of English.

Velez-Ibanez, C. 1995. "The Challenge of Funds of Knowledge in Urban Arenas: Another Way of Understanding the Learning Resources of Poor Mexicano Households in the United States Southwest." In *The Anthropology of Lower Income Urban Enclaves*, ed. Judith N. Freidenberg, 253–281. New York: Annals of the New York Academy of Sciences, Volume 749.

Velez-Ibanez, C. and J.B. Greenberg. 1992. "Formation and Transformation of Funds of Knowledge Among U.S. Mexican Households: Contexts for Educational Reformation in the Southwest Region. *Anthropology and Education Quarterly* (23) 4: 313–335.

Visser, M. 1991. *The Rituals of Dinner*. New York: Penguin.

Washington, M.H. 1991. *Memory of Kin*. New York: Doubleday Anchor Books. Weisfeld, E. 1991. *The Book of Life: A Celebration of Family*. New York: District 3 Magnet Project.

Wells, G. 1986. "The Language Experience of 5-year-old Children at Home and at School." In *The Social Construction of Literacy*, ed. J. Cook-Gumperz, 69–93. New York: Cambridge University Press.

Wickens, E. 1993. "Penny's Question." *Young Children* (March).

Wigginton, E. 1972. *The Foxfire Book*. New York: Doubleday Anchor Books.

Zeitlin, S.J. 1993. "How I Almost Never Got Born." *Citylore* (3): 15.

Zeitlin, S.J., A.J. Kotkin, and H.C. Baker. 1982. *A Celebration of American Family Folklore*. Cambridge, MA: Yellow Moon Press.

Zimmerman, W. 1988. *How to Tape Instant Oral Biographies*. New York: Guarionex Press.

Zingher, G. 1990. *At the Pirate Academy: Adventures with Language in the Library Media Center*. Chicago and London: American Library Association.

Zinsser, W. 1987. *Inventing the Truth: The Art and Craft of Memoir*. Boston, MA: Houghton Mifflin.

Preface to the Picture Book Bibliography

Why do some families regard certain picture books in heartfelt ways? How might such books reflect the values and concerns of a family or illuminate a family's history? Prized picture books often become family treasures, heirlooms of a sort, to be kept, shared, and passed on to the next generation. Some may be rare first editions, autographed and gold leafed. Others may be weathered, slightly unbound, with damaged spines. Whatever their condition, picture books can help sustain family life, providing a sense of continuity and a source of delight. The mere pulling out of such a book can evoke in children a burst of emotion and a tingling effect: a chuckle, a gasp, a sigh. Almost magically, children will shift gears and become listeners so that they can once again enjoy the obstinate Pierre bellowing, "I don't care!" or the Teeny Tiny Woman shuddering under her covers as the rising voice in the cupboard demands, "Give me my bone!"

These "heirloom" books are like comfort foods, for they can soothe and nourish children and help them feel safe and relaxed. They become part of a family's legacy. Often, for children, they are associated with intimate moments spent with important caregivers. They may connect children to other times and worlds; their texts may be written in various languages. For grown-ups, reading such books aloud can strike deep chords that reopen the past, reminding them of their earliest joys and anxieties, and enabling them to share pieces of their own childhood.

The first time an adult shares a Baba Yaga or Anansi story with a child can become a joyful literary event, a story celebration, a rite of passage in which the child receives one of the most cherished gifts of a particular culture.

Children enjoy identifying and sharing these books with each other, examining their contents, illustrations, copyright dates, and places of publication. Where did these books originate? How long have they been in families? Why do they have such power? Children might want to help repair and rebind their books, or create striking new covers or jackets.

The picture books that are annotated in the following bibliography can be used to stimulate children's thinking about the possibilities of family life. They raise questions that provoke all kinds of exchange. What holds families together? How do they establish common ground? What are their traditions, stories, songs, jokes, recipes, and games? How do we identify a family's particular character, humor, or style? How do family members support and/or inhibit each other? How do they express their joy, grief, frustration, anger?

A number of books portray families as they begin the day. Are mornings fun and relaxed, or edgy and rushed? Are there certain chores and routines? Cynthia Rylant in *When I Was Young In the Mountains* fondly recalls Appalachian mornings, "heated baths in round hot tubs," and "crumbled cornbread in buttermilk." In *By the Dawn's Early Light*, Ackerman depicts a nightshift working mother enjoying a warm interlude with her two kids as they wait for the sun to rise. This is their only morning time for sharing affection, touching base, and catching up on all that has happened.

Ira Sleeps Over, by Waber, can spark children's awareness of the variation in everyday routines of neighboring families. How do the routines compare to their own? What happens in the evening, at night? Do all the family members eat together? Who clears the table? Who washes the dishes? Do they have special foods for bedtime snacks? Do the adults sing lullabies or read from chapter books? Is the light on in the hall? How far away is the bathroom?

What are the lessons of home? What skills are acquired and how are they passed down? Do children learn these skills through instruction, observation, or example? Grandparents or other elders generally play an important role in transmitting knowledge. Often they are able to cushion a child's frustrations by creating a circle of intimacy and warmth. Esperanza, the Guatemalan girl in Castaneda's book *Abuela's Weave*, begins to master the complex process of weaving as she listens to her grandmother: "Pull back. Make it jolt so the threads stay close, like family." Little Soo in Tombert's book *Grandfather Tang's Story* learns the magic of tangrams, an ancient Chinese art form that is a special kind of storytelling, as she watches her grandfather arrange its seven wooden pieces into a fox, a rabbit, a crocodile.

How do families cope with loss, express their pain, begin to heal? *A Chair for My Mother*, Vera B. Williams's book about a family's resilience and tenacity after a devastating fire, acknowledges that no family is immune from struggle and crisis. The chair in this story is a symbol of hope and shared dreams. The book illustrates how family members express their concern for each other and how children contribute to restoring order. In discussing a book like this one, some children may choose to describe troubling times in their own families and how setbacks were dealt with and overcome.

Many kinds of stories are passed down in a family: rescue tales, courtship tales, tales of irony and poignancy, tales with and without heroes or heroines. Each family has its history and lore, episodes and stories that resurface time and again, recreating and preserving its extraordinary moments. Picture books can be excellent incentives for children to interview family members and elicit stories tied to specific themes. Stolz's *Storm in the Night* portrays a grandfather and grandson who deal with a darkened house and a threatening storm by exchanging tales and banter. As they sit on their front porch swing, the two admit some of their fears to each other. There is an intimacy between them, a trust, an appreciation of exaggerated and shared humor. Polacco's *Thunder Cake* describes a grandmother's and granddaughter's efforts to bake a cake before a storm begins. There are errands to run, ingredients to collect, concrete things to do. Despite crashes and booms from the sky, the two remain focused on their special project. Both these books offer wonderful adult models who are playful and respectful in the ways they interact with children. Both use imaginative means to engage children and help them work through anxieties.

Books such as Waters's *Lion Dancer* and Delacre's *Vejigante* can inspire children to tap into family stories about people dressing up in traditional clothes or creating their own costumes for cultural celebrations. These books show not only how festivities strengthen family unity and provide joyful vehicles for coming together, but also how costumes give children license to take risks, try out new personas, and even revel with beasties and ghosts and creatures of the dark.

Picture books can be used to begin family story collections about bets and dares, bullies, celebrities, encounters with animals, special and secret places, weddings and feasts, contests and prizes, or childhood indignities. Family-themed books might also be used as springboards for creative excursions. Clifton's book *The Lucky Stone*, about a keepsake that has linked and helped protect family members across generations, might lead children to create a "family museum" with a variety of lucky family treasures: charms, photos, lockets, locks of hair, wishbones, horseshoes, pennies, or crystals. Children can explore why these objects are valued. How were they found or acquired? Wahl's *Little Eight John* can be used to promote inquiry into family superstitions. In what regions or countries did they originate? The antics of the mean, mischievous, toad-kicking boy in Wahl's book can stimulate children to collect family superstitions. The children can then develop little plays that describe how these superstitions might have come into being.

Why do some people knock on wood? Why would others never whistle backstage, or in a graveyard? Children can illustrate such family superstitions by making giant-sized posters.

Galimoto, by Karen Lynn Williams, describes a South African boy's inventiveness and resourcefulness in collecting wire to build his miniature vehicle. This story may spur children to develop an exhibit of childmade toys, such as tops, kites, apple core dolls, whistles, and their own galimotos. What were the toys their grandparents and parents created? Some children may wish to design and produce a toy catalog of these homemade inventions. *Uncle Nacho's Hat*, by Rohmer, might excite kids to bring in unusual hats from home: a Western hat, a high silk hat, beret, beanie, crown, or fanciful bonnet. They could become the Hatbox Players and develop improvised plays, using these hats to suggest characters and situations.

The picture books mentioned here and the others listed in the bibliography can be touchstones for stimulating family study and launching thematic journeys. Celebrating family strengths and linking children in positive ways to their cultures, they teach that families are varied, dynamic, and evolving. Each has its own way of seeing the world, its own history, and its own unfolding story.

—*Gary Zingher*

Annotated Bibliography of Picture Books

This bibliography is not intended to be exhaustive but, rather, suggestive of books that support the family stories projects described in the preceding chapters. Sincere and sensitive arguments have been made to me by colleagues on all sides of the debate over whether and/or how to use children's books that represent, and are written by, members of the dominant cultural group. I appreciate the need for teachers and families to remain alert to the issue, but it is not within the scope of this book to enter the debate. Accordingly, this bibliography is based on what teachers have told me they found most useful.

One approach to diversifying the picture books available to children is offered by The Children's Book Press in San Francisco, California (Tel. 415-995-2200), which has published award-winning multicultural literature for children for more than twenty years, including a range of bilingual picture books in Spanish, Vietnamese, Cambodian, Chinese, and Korean, for K–6 students.

Each section of the bibliography corresponds to a chapter in the book, with selections listed alphabetically by title. Except where indicated, the place of publication is New York. Starred annotations are from the annual reviews published by the Child Study Association Children's Book Committee.

BOOKS REVIEWED IN GARY ZINGHER'S PREFACE TO THIS BIBLIOGRAPHY

ACKERMAN, KAREN. *By the Dawn's Early Light.* 1994. Atheneum.

ARNOLD, KATYA. *Baba Yaga.* 1993. North-South Books.

CASTANEDA, OMAR. *Abuela's Weave.* 1994. Publishers Group West.

CLIFTON, LUCILLE. *The Lucky Stone.* 1978. Delacorte.

DALACRE, L. *Vejigante Masquerade.* 1993. Scholastic.

MCDERMOTT, GERALD. *Anansi.* 1972. Holt, Rinehart and Winston.

POLACCO, PATRICIA. *Thunder Cake.* 1990. Putnam.

ROHMER, H. *Uncle Nacho's Hat.* 1990. Ingram.

RYLANT, CYNTHIA. *When I Was Young in the Mountains.* 1982. Dutton.

SENDAK, MAURICE. *Pierre: A Cautionary Tale.* 1962. Harper.

SEULING, BARBARA. *The Teeny Tiny Woman: An Old English Ghost Tale.* 1976. Viking.

STOLZ, MARY. *Storm in the Night.* 1988. Harper and Row.

TOMPERT, ANN. *Grandfather Tang's Story.* 1990. Crown.

WABER, BERNARD. *Ira Sleeps Over.* 1972. Houghton Mifflin.

WAHL, JAN. *Little Eight John.* 1980. Dutton.

WATERS, KATE. *The Lion Dancer.* 1990. Scholastic.

WILLIAMS, KAREN LYNN. *Galimoto.* 1990. Lothrop, Lee and Shepard.

WILLIAMS, VERA B. *A Chair for My Mother.* 1982. Greenwillow.

CHAPTER 1

Books that Portray Family Structures

Always My Dad, by Sharon Dennis Wyeth, ill. by Raul Colon. 1995. Knopf.
  A young African-American girl spends the summer on her grandparents' farm, where she and her younger brothers share special moments that make up for the times when their father's work takes him away from home.

*By the Dawn's Early Light, by Karen Ackerman, ill. by Catherine Stock. 1994. Atheneum.
  A grandmother cares for two children while their mother works at night. Pictures convey the story's warmth.

Daddy's Roommate, written and ill. by Michael Wilhoite. 1990. Alyson
Wonderland: Boston.
Spare, good text describes the life of gay partners and their child.

*Friday's Journey, written and ill. by Ken Rush. 1994. Orchard.
*Riding the subway with his dad for his weekend visit, Chris remembers all the
places they used to go when the family was together.*

*Homeless, written and photographed by Bernard Wolf. 1995. Orchard.
*A tender tale told by a homeless eight-year-old boy. Vivid photographs evoke
the tenacity of a family's spirit.*

*Like Jake and Me, by Mavis Jukes, ill. by Lloyd Bloom. 1984. Knopf.
*A young boy is finally able to help his stepfather in this humorous and loving
family story. Beautiful, bright illustrations enhance the text.*

My Mother's House, My Father's House, by C.B. Christiansen, ill. by Irene
Trivas. 1989. Atheneum.
*Depicts a child's feelings about loving parents in a common family situation
with warmth and honesty.*

*Priscilla Twice, written and ill. by Judith Caseley. 1995. Greenwillow.
*Priscilla is beginning to learn what it is like to have two homes, one with
Daddy and one with Mama. Illustrations support the story's emotions.*

The Relatives Came, by Cynthia Rylant, ill. by Stephen Gammell. 1985.
Bradbury.
*A fine celebration of a family reunion in rustic rural Virgina is full of fun,
family love, and support.*

*Shoes Like Miss Alice's, by Angela Johnson, ill. by Ken Page. 1995. Orchard.
*A child's reluctance to accept a new baby-sitter turns into appreciation of the
pleasure Miss Alice brings to the day.*

*Through Moon and Stars and Night Skies, by Ann Turner, ill. by James
Graham Hale. 1990. Harper and Row.
*A little boy adopted by a new momma and poppa remembers how he traveled
to them from a far-off land.*

*Way Home, by Libby Holman, ill. by Gregory Rogers. 1994. Crown.
*The tender story of a homeless boy who rescues a cat and carries it through the
city to his hangout. Powerful, somber illustrations.*

Who's in a Family? by Robert Skutch, ill. by Laura Nienhaus. 1995. Tricycle Press.
Nonstereotyped portraits of families working and playing together are juxtaposed with various family structures from the animal world.

Birth and Naming

Knots on a Counting Rope, by Bill Martin, Jr., and John Archambault, ill. by Ted Rand. 1987. Henry Holt.
A blind Indian boy and his grandfather retell the story of his birth and naming.

On the Day I Was Born, by Debbi Chocolate, ill. by Melodye Rosales. 1995. Scholastic.
Aunts, uncles, and grandparents join father and mother to welcome and bestow wondrous gifts on a newborn infant. Age-old African traditions combine with newfound family rituals.

Generations

The Keeping Quilt, written and ill. by Patricia Polacco. 1988. Simon & Schuster.
A quilt made from old clothes is used through four generations, from Russia to America.

*The Lucky Stone, by Lucille Clifton, ill. by Dale Payson. 1978. Delacorte.
"Good luck" stories of three generations in a black family, from slavery to freedom, told to a little girl by her great-grandmother. Expressive illustrations.

Siblings

*Do Like Kyla, by Angela Johnson, ill. by James E. Ransome. 1990. Orchard.
Kyla leads the way all day, but at one important moment she imitates her younger sister.

*Jamaica Tag-A-Long, by Juanita Havill, ill. by Anne Sibley O'Brien. 1989. Scholastic.
Rejected by her brother's team, Jamaica learns not to shut out a younger child.

Spinky Sulks, written and ill. by William Steig. 1988. Farrar, Strauss and Giroux.
  Loving parents and siblings try to counter Spinky's resentments, which eventually dissolve into a glorious surprise.

With My Brother/Con Mi Hermano, by Eileen Roe, ill, by Robert Casila. 1991. Bradbury.
  A bilingual account of a warm relationship.

Troubling Times

A Chair for My Mother, by Vera B. Williams. 1982. Greenwillow.
  After a fire that destroys all of their possessions, a poor family works hard to save enough money to buy a "wonderful, beautiful, fat, soft armchair for mom."

Tikvah Means Hope, by Patricia Polacco. 1994. Doubleday.
  After a devastating fire in the hills of Oakland, California, during Sukkot, a Jewish family and their neighbors find symbols of hope amidst the ashes.

Death of a Beloved Relative

Losing Uncle Tim, by Mary Kate Jordan, ill. by Judith Freidman. 1991. Whitman, Morton Grove, IL.
  A young boy is helped to understand, and become reconciled to, the death from AIDS of a beloved uncle. Sensitive illustrations.

Nadia the Willful, by Sue Alexander, ill. by Lloyd Bloom. 1983. Pantheon.
  The universal feeling that a person remembered is not lost shines through this moving tale, which is matched by softly drawn illustrations.

The New King, by Doreen Rappaport, ill. by E.B. Lewis. 1995. Dial.
  Through wise counsel, the little Malagasy prince's angry reaction to his father's death is turned to helpfulness. Watercolors capture the setting.

CHAPTER 2

Grandpa Was a Cowboy, by Silky Sullivan, ill. by Bert Dodson. 1996. Orchard.
  Grandpa's tales of the past give his orphaned grandson a deep sense of his own heritage.

Isla, by Arthur Dorros, ill. by Elisa Kleven. 1995. Dutton.
> *A young girl visits her grandmother's native Caribbean island through the magic of Abuela's stories. Glorious illustrations.*

May'naise Sandwiches and Sunshine Tea, by Sandra Belton, ill. by Gail Gordon Carter. 1994. Four Winds.
> *Photographs and souvenirs of family and family history make grandma's scrapbook of "rememberies" a treasure house of hope and imagination.*

Sitti's Secrets, by Naomi Shihab Nye, ill. by Nancy Carpenter. 1994. Four Winds.
> *Sitti visits her grandmother in Palestine and learns about family and cultural ties. Magnificent illustrations.*

Tales of a Gambling Grandmother, by Dayal Kaur Khalsa. 1986. Crown.
> *Recalling the advice of his warm, independent grandmother, the author appreciates her strong influence on his life.*

Tanya's Reunion, by Valerie Flournoy, ill. by Jerry Pinkney. 1995. Dial.
> *Tanya joins her grandma as the family prepares for a reunion on the farm, where memories and stories of the past are shared. Warm, detailed watercolors.*

What's in Aunt Mary's Room, by Elizabeth Howard, ill. by Cedric Lucas. 1996. Clarion.
> *Family history discovered by Sarah and her sister through the "things to save and things to keep" they find in Aunt Mary's room.*

Your Dad Was Just Like You, written and ill. by Dolores Johnson. 1993. Macmillan.
> *Peter's grandfather tells him a story about his father's boyhood, which helps him better understand his father.*

CHAPTER 3
Storytelling

Abiyoyo, by Pete Seeger, ill. by Michael Hays. 1986. Macmillan.
> *An African folk tale of a terrible giant conquered by a boy's song. Magnificent illustrations. Includes music.*

The Chalk Doll, by Charlotte Pomerantz, ill, by Frane Lessac. 1989.
Lippincott.
When Rose has a cold, her mother tells her stories of her own happy though impoverished childhood.

Homeplace, by Anne Shelby, ill. by Wendy Anderson Halperin. 1995.
Orchard.
A child hears about the history of her house and the two centuries of ancestors who have lived in it and loved it. Spectacular illustrations.

Nursery Tales Around the World, retold by Judy Sierra, ill. by Stefano Vitale.
1996. Clarion.
Eighteen tales, grouped in threes according to similar themes. Illustrations capture the flavor of the country of origin.

Papa Tells Chita a Story, by Elizabeth Fitzgerald Howard, ill. by Floyd
Cooper. 1995. Simon and Schuster.
Chita loves her father's storytelling, especially the story he weaves from his experience in the Spanish-American War.

The Patchwork Quilt, by Valerie Flournoy, ill. by Jerry Pinkney. 1985. Dial.
Tender relationships and memories emerge in the making of the quilt by a beloved grandmother.

The Seal Mother, written and ill. by Mordecai Gerstein. 1986. Dial.
Grand folktale of Scottish origin about the marriage of a fisherman and a seal, and about their son. Beautiful illustrations.

Tell Me a Story Mama, by Angela Johnson, ill. by D. Soman. 1989 New York:
Orchard Books.
A little girl asks for a familiar bedtime story, which she herself then tells.

Poetry

Families: Poems Celebrating the African American Experience, selected by
Dorothy S. Strickland and Michael R. Strickland, ill. by John Ward.
1994. Boyds Mill.
Rich language and images infuse this anthology of poems and will delight all children.

Fathers, Mothers, Sisters, Brothers, by Mary Ann Hoberman, ill. by Marylin Hafner. 1991. Little Brown.
Verses on family experiences familiar to all children. Amusing illustrations.

Inner Chimes, selected by Bobbye S. Goldstein, ill. by Jane Breskin Zalben. 1993. Boyds Mills.
A thoughtful collection of poems about poetry—how poets write, what makes a poem, how poetry inspires.

Mama Rocks, Papa Sings, by Nancy Van Laan, ill. by Roberta Smith. 1995. Knopf.
A rollicking, rhyming tale of a family in Haiti. Glimpses of everyday life among families and neighbors amidst the natural beauty of the island.

The Matzah That Papa Brought Home, by Fran Manushkin, ill. by Ned Bittinger. 1995. Scholastic.
A Passover holiday story in the rhyming style of "The House That Jack Built," with realistic, detailed illustrations that illuminate traditions celebrated through the generations.

Skip Across the Ocean: Nursery Rhymes from Around the World, collected by Floella Benjamin, ill. by Sheila Moxley. 1995. Orchard.
Rhymes and lullabies from all over the world, some in their original language with translation. Colorful, stylized illustrations to match.

Sing a Song of Popcorn, by Beatrice Schenk de Regniers and Eva Moore, ill. by Caldecott Winners. 1988. Scholastic.
A happy mix of old and new poems, with illustrations by award-winning artists.

CHAPTER 4
Stories

The Last Dragon, by Susan Miho Nunes, ill. by Chris K. Soentpiet. 1995. New York: Clarion Books.
Summering with his great-aunt in Chinatown, Peter discovers a tattered dragon and restores it. Vibrant pictures capture the milieu.

Night Visitors, written and ill. by Ed Young. 1995. Philomel.
In this Chinese tale, a man's dream awakens his reverence for all creatures, even ants. Poetic illustrations match the tenderness of the text.

The Stonecutter, written and ill. by Demi. 1995. Crown.
   A stonecutter keeps wishing to be something else until this old Chinese tale comes full circle. Splendid illustrations.

Yang the Third and Her Impossible Family, by Namioka Lensey, ill. by Kees de Kiefte. 1995. Little Brown.
   Yang lives in an American city, Seattle. Her family's traditional Chinese ways make it difficult for her to make a new American friend. Appealing illustrations.

Memoir

Aunt Flossie's Hats (and Crab Cakes Later), by Elizabeth F. Howard, paintings by James Ransome. 1991. Clarion.
   Lyrical, authentic memoir of the author's ninety-eight-year-old aunt. Oil paintings enhance the text.

Been to Yesterdays, by Lee Bennett Hopkins, ill. by Charlene Rendeiro. 1995. Wordsong.
   Easily read poems, with photographs of the poet's childhood and family life.

The Days Before Now, adapted by Joan W. Blos, ill. by Thomas B. Allen. 1994. Simon and Schuster.
   Scenes from the life of Margaret Wise Brown, celebrated author of Goodnight Moon, *as a child and adult in New York City and Long Island.*

Hair=Pelitos, by Sandra Cisneros, ill. by Terry Ybanez. 1994. Knopf.
   A girl describes individual differences in the hair of each person in her family.

When Frank Was Four, written and ill. by Alison Lester. 1996. Houghton Mifflin.
   An album of humorous, charming pictures of children, ages four through seven. Brief captions highlight the hurdles and achievements of childhood.

When I Was Little: A Four-Year-Old's Memoir of Her Youth, by Jamie Lee Curtis, ill. by Laura Cornell. 1994. HarperCollins.
   At first, there were not many things a child could do; now she can do a lot.

When I Was Young in the Moutains, by Cynthia Rylant, ill. by Diane Goode. 1982. Dutton
A poetic, sensitive memoir of childhood in Appalachia. Illustrations evoke the setting.

CHAPTER 5

*Everybody Bakes Bread, by Norah Dooley, ill. by Peter J. Thornton. 1996. Carolrhoda Books: Minneapolis.

*Everybody Cooks Rice, by Norah Dooley, ill. by Peter J. Thornton. 1991. Minneapolis: Carolrhoda Books.
Carrie samples wonderful ethnic foods on her trips around her neighborhood. Lovely illustrations and recipes appear in both these books. 1984. Boston: Houghton Mifflin.

The Gingerbread Boy, by Paul Galdrone. 1975. Clarion.
Charming rendition of a traditional tale.

Hot Cross Buns and Other Street Cries, by John Langstaff. 1978. Atheneum.
Folk songs and sayings related to food.

*How My Parents Learned to Eat, by Ina R. Friedman, ill. by Allen Say. 1984. Boston: Houghton Mifflin.
How the author's American father and Japanese mother met and learned to respect one another's customs. Tender illustrations.

Johnny Cake, by Joseph Jacobs. 1933. Putnam.
A classic trickster tale.

The Magic Porridge Pot, by Paul Galdrone. 1976. Houghton Mifflin.
Another of Galdrone's imaginative retellings of a well-known folktale.

*Peas and Honey: Recipes for Kids (with a Pinch of Poetry), written and compiled by Kimberly Colen, ill. by Mandy Victor. 1995. Boyds Mill.
Multicultural offering of recipes and poetry, colorfully illustrated.

*Stone Soup, retold by John Warren Stewig, ill. by Margot Tomes. 1991. Holiday.
A new telling of an old tale: A clever girl tricks stingy villagers into preparing a meal for her.

Strega Nona, retold and ill. by Tomie de Paola. 1975. Prentice Hall.
   Anthony couldn't stop the magic pasta pot from nearly drowning the whole town in spaghetti.

Sunday Potatoes, Monday Potatoes, by Vicky Shiefman. 1994. Simon and Schuster.
   A poor family eats potatoes every day of the week except on Saturday, when they eat their special potato pudding.

CHAPTER 6

Across the Wide Dark Sea: The Mayflower Journey, by Jean Van Leeuwen, ill. by Thomas B. Allen. 1995. Dial.
   A young boy aboard the Mayflower experiences the dangers and satisfactions of the Pilgrims' journey. Evocative pastel drawings.

Dia's Story Cloth, by Dia Cha, stitched by Chue and Nhia Thao Cha. 1996. Lee and Low.
   The life and migrations of the Hmong people through Asia and ultimately to the United States, extracted from a magnificent embroidery.

Coming To America: The Story of Immigration, by Betsy Maestro, ill. by Susannah Ryan. 1996. Scholastic.
   An overview of immigration from the first nomads to the present day. Colorfully illustrated.

Ebony Sea, by Irene Smalls, ill. by Jon Onye Lockard. 1996. Longmeadow Press.
   Africans (Ebos) arriving in America select death with dignity over slavery in this boldly illustrated, lyrical tale.

How Many Days to America? by Eve Bunting, ill. by Beth Peck. 1988. Clarion.
   A fine book about an immigration journey. For Thanksgiving holiday reading.

Immigrant Girl, by Harvey Brett. 1987. Holiday.
   Becky, whose family has emigrated from Russia to avoid being persecuted as Jews, finds growing up in New York City in 1910 a vivid and exciting experience.

Grandfather's Journey, written and ill. by Allen Say. 1993. Houghton Mifflin.
Glowing pictures illuminate the memories of the author's grandfather and his life in America and Japan.

Halmoni and the Picnic, by Sook Nyul Choi, ill. by Karen M. Dugan. 1993. Houghton Mifflin.
Yunni worries that her classmates will make fun of her grandmother, who has just emigrated from Korea.

In America, written and ill. by Marissa Moss. 1993. Penguin.
Walter learns what a hard decision it was for Grandpa to leave his brother to come to America. Would Walter be as brave? Touching and funny.

Molly's Pilgrim, by Barbara Cohen, ill. by M.J. Deraney. 1983. Lothrop.
Sensitive story of an immigrant Jewish girl and her American classmates who learn the meaning of Thanksgiving.

Morning Girl, by Michael Dorris 1994. Little Brown.
Immigration as seen from the persepctive of a Taino girl, who lived before the arrival of Columbus.

My Grandmother's Journey, by John Cech, ill. by Sharon McGinley. 1991. Bradbury.
Grandmother's story of life in Europe and the journey to the United States after World War II.

Peppe the Lamplighter, by Elisa Bartone, ill. by Ted Levin. 1993. Lothrop, Lee and Shepard.
An interesting and realistic story of immigrants in New York's Little Italy early in the twentieth century. Splendid illustrations.

What You Know First, by Patricia MacLachlan, ill. by Barry Moser. 1995. New York: HarperCollins.
As a family gets ready to move to a new house and a new land they've never seen, the older child comes to terms with leaving what she knew first. Magnificent engravings inspired by photographs from both the author's and the illustrator's family albums.

The Wooden Doll, by Susan Bonner. 1991. Lothrop.
Stephanie is finally old enough to learn the story of her grandfather's wooden doll.

Yagua Days, by Cruz Martel, ill. by Jerry Pinkney 1987. Dial.
  A New York boy visits relatives in Puerto Rico and shares their gaiety and lively games.

CHAPTER 7

How Does It Feel to Be Old? by Norma Farber, ill. by Trina Schart Hyman. 1979. Dutton.
  An old woman explains some of the pleasures and pains of being old to her granddaughter. Realistic, positive, poignant.

I Know a Lady, by Charlotte Zolotow, ill. by James Stevenson. 1984. Greenwillow.
  The story of an elderly neighbor woman who shares her garden, gives Halloween treats, and knows the names of the children's pets.

Miss Maggie, by Cynthia Rylant, ill. by Thomas Di Grazia. 1983. Dutton.
  A young boy makes friends with an old woman who lives in a log house at the end of the pasture.

My Great Grandpa Joe, by Marilyn Gelfand, photographs by Rosemarie Hausherr. 1986. Four Winds.
  Through a photo album, a young girl learns about her great-grandfather and about aging.

The Old, Old Man and the Very Little Boy, by Kristine L. Franklin. 1992. Atheneum.
  As he listens to Old Father's stories each day, a little boy asks if his friend has ever been young, but only after he has grown old himself, does he understand Old Father's answer.

When Artie Was Little, by Harriet Berg Schwartz, ill. by Thomas B. Allen. 1996. Knopf.
  Artie, an old man, tells the neighborhood children stories of his childhood. Pastels capture the past.

Wilfrid Gordon McDonald Partridge, by Mem Fox, ill. by Julie Vivas. 1984. Kane/Miller.
  A young boy begins a project of finding memories for his favorite friend in the old peoples' home next door.

CHAPTER 8

Amelia Bedelia's Family Album, by Peggy Parrish. 1988. Avon, Camelot.
    Amelia Bedelia's relatives are just as funny as she is.

*Brown Angels, by Walter Dean Myers. 1993. Harper Collins.
    *A collection of poems in tribute to African-American children, with early
    twentieth-century photographs.*

How the Other Half Lives, photographs of Jacob Riis. 1996. St. Martin's Press.
    *Photographs and text describing life and families on New York City's Lower
    East Side at the end of the twentieth century, as seen through the eyes of a
    well-known social reformer.*

Lincoln: A Photobiography, by Russell Freedman. 1987. Houghton Mifflin.
    The life of Abraham Lincoln told through photographs and text.

*Out of the Dump: Writings and Photographs by Children from Guatemala, edit-
    ed by Kristine L. Franklin and Nancy McGirr. 1996. Lothrop, Lee and
    Shepard.
    *A disturbingly honest view of life in and around the garbage dump in the cen-
    ter of Guatemala. To be used with adult guidance.*

Prairie Visions, by Pam Conrad. 1991. HarperTrophy.
    *Biography and photography record the lives of turn-of-the-century pioneer
    families in Custer County, Nebraska. Photographs from the Nebraska State
    Historical Society.*

Resources for Teachers

ORGANIZATIONS

Center for Folk Arts in Education
Bank Street College of Education
603 West 111th Street
New York, N.Y. 10025

In 1994, Bank Street College and City Lore received a four-year Challenge Grant to develop a folk arts program in the schools and a multicultural resource center for teachers. The center helps teachers reach local artists and musicians in the communities who are willing to bring their skills to the classroom; it also introduces teachers to a range of curriculum materials through its multimedia library and computer center, its publications, and its catalogue of resources.

City Lore: The New York Center for Urban Folk Culture
72 East First Street
New York, N.Y. 10003
Fax # (212) 529-5062

City Lore presents festivals, exhibitions, and radio shows on the folk arts in New York City. It sends artists into schools, collaborates with Bank Street College's arts in education program, and documents folkways in New York through its publications and contributions to public library archives. Members receive a journal; books and other publications are available on request.

Elders Share the Arts
52 Willoughby Street
Brooklyn, N.Y. 11201

ESTA is a community arts organization that trains performance artists to coordinate intergenerational oral history and living theater projects that bring children and elders together in schools and senior centers. Their publications include a newsletter and a guide book for schools and community-based groups.

Global Village Video
431 Broome Street
New York, N.Y. 10013

Global Village makes and distributes videotapes of family storytellers and intergenerational projects in schools. They publish a catalogue of their resources.

Henry Street Settlement: Arts in Education Program
466 Grand Street
New York, N.Y. 10002

Henry Street's Arts in Education program runs parent storytelling workshops in schools and publishes yearly anthologies of family stories gathered by and from participants.

National Storytelling Association
P.O.Box 309
Jonesborough, T.N. 37659
Fax # (423) 753-9331

The NSA holds annual storytelling festivals at Jonesborough, sponsors conferences, and publishes resource catalogues and a directory of professional storytellers, books, audiotapes, and compact discs. They will help find storytellers with a family focus to work in schools.

Teachers and Writers Collaborative
5 Union Square West (5th floor)
New York, N.Y. 10003

Teachers and Writers provides artists and oral historians to work with teachers in classrooms. They hold educational conferences and publish books and other resources for teachers.

CONSULTANTS

Dr. Judith Pasamanick
360 First Avenue (Apt. 5 F)
New York, N.Y. 10010

Dr. Pasamanick founded and directed the NEH Summer Institutes in Folklore at Bank Street College.

Dr. Michele Sola, Director of Special Projects
Manhattan Country School
7 East 96th Street
New York, N.Y. 10128

MCS runs workshops all over the country for teachers interested in experiencing its flagship Family Study curriculum.

All the teachers listed in the extended acknowledgments of this book are available for consultation. They can be reached through their schools and organizations or through the author.

ANTHOLOGIES OF FAMILY STORIES

A Celebration of American Family Folklore. Steven Zeitlin, Amy J. Kotkin, Holly Cutting Baker. 1982. Yellow Moon Press.
If you select only one book, this is the one to get. It contains hundreds of stories collected by a team of folklorists from people who came from all over the country to attend the Festival of American Folklife, sponsored by the Smithsonian in Washington, D.C., during the summers of 1973 to 1976. It includes more than fourteen categories of family stories, commentaries by the editors, and a section on how to collect your own family folklore.

The Foxfire Book. Eliot Wigginton. 1972. Doubleday.
High school students in Appalachia, under the guidance of a dedicated teacher, present information on "affairs of plain living" that they collected from elders in their community.

The Speaking Forest, 1996. Children's Workshop School. Community School District One. New York, NY.
An anthology of family stories told by adults in the families of children attending CWS and by teachers and staff at the school.

READINGS WITH A FOCUS ON FOLKLORE

Brewer's Dictionary of Phrase and Fable. Ivor H. Evans (ed.). 1970. Cassell.

The Prentice Hall Encyclopedia of World Proverbs. Wolfgang Mieder. 1978. Prentice Hall.

Clever Cooks: A Concoction of Stories, Charms, Recipes and Riddles. Ellin Greene. 1973. Lothrop, Lee and Shepard.

GUIDES TO COLLECTING FAMILY STORIES AND ORAL HISTORIES

Books

Family History Activity Pack. DK Publishing. New York. 1996.
Hands-on activities for doing family history research with young children. Includes pocket camera, activity book, family tree poster, stickers, and games.

Like It Was: A Complete Guide to Writing Oral History. Cynthia Stokes Brown. Teachers and Writers Collaborative. New York. 1986.

Telling Your Own Stories. Donald Davis. August House. Little Rock, AR. 1993.

To Our Children's Children. Bob Greene and D. G. Fulford. Doubleday. 1993.

Stories: The Family Legacy. Richard Stone. StoryWork Institute. Maitland, FL. 1994.

News Groups on the Internet

There are 17 genealogy news groups based in the United States. Call the Usenet Genealogy Newsgroups-Hotlink to Newsgroups (**http://dcn.davis. ca.us/~feefhs/newsgrps.htm**) to get a listing or, using a search engine, type in the words *genealogy* and *newsgroups.* You will get a message center. Post a message to the news group and return to find personal replies posted from around the world.

Home Pages: Using a search engine, type in the word *genealogy* and add a specific reference such as Irish, Jewish, African-American, or even your own last name. You will get a list of related home pages (possibly hundreds), with content ranging from how-to information to someone's family tree.

GUIDELINES FOR INTERGENERATIONAL PROJECTS

Generating Community, by Susan Perlstein and Jeff Bliss. 1994. The Print Center, 225 Varick St., New York, NY. (212) 206-8465.
A guide to creating intergenerational partnerships through the expressive arts, with photos and text, produced by Elders Share the Arts.

Nourishing the Heart, by Shari Davis and Benny Ferdman. 1993. City Lore and Creative Ways. New York.
A guide to intergenerational arts projects in the schools.

FILMS AND PHOTOGRAPHY EXHIBITS

J.T., CBS Television. 1969. 51 minutes.
The life of a troubled boy in a struggling Harlem family becomes more hopeful when he cares for and becomes attached to a street cat.

Sugar Cane Alley, by Euzhan Palcy. France. 1984. 103 minutes.
A coming-of-age story, set in Martinique, about the relationship between a boy and his grandmother who works in the sugar cane fields. Fifth grade and up.

The Little Fugitive, directed by Ray Ashley. Burstyn. 1953. 75 minutes.
Academy Award–winning film about a boy who runs away to Coney Island when he mistakenly thinks he has killed his brother. A survival theme. Third grade and up.

It's Elementary, directed by Academy Award–winning filmmaker Debra Chasnoff. This documentary for educators and parents includes some classrooms from schools described in this book; the film makes a compelling case for incorporating gay issues into antibias education in the classroom. Accompanied by teaching guide.

Other: Portraits of Multiracial Families, a ready-to-hang, museum-quality traveling photograph-text exhibit by Gigi Kaeser and Peggy Gillespie. Featured in *Teaching Tolerance Magazine,* it includes twenty diverse families formed through interracial relationships and/or adoption. Two versions are available, one with text suitable for kindergarten through sixth grade students, and one for older students and adults. Accompanied by a resource guide that includes the complete text, curriculum ideas, booklists, census guides, and several relevant articles. Contact Peggy Gillespie, P.O. Box 1216, Amherst, MA 01004-1216. Phone: 413-256-0502. Fax: 413-253-3977. E-Mail: FamPhoto@aol.com.